Praise of
Motherhood

Praise of Motherhood

Phil Jourdan

Winchester, UK
Washington, USA

First published by Zero Books, 2012
Zero Books is an imprint of John Hunt Publishing Ltd., Laurel House, Station Approach,
Alresford, Hants, SO24 9JH, UK
office1@o-books.net
www.o-books.com

For distributor details and how to order please visit the 'Ordering' section on our website.

Text copyright: Phil Jourdan 2011

ISBN: 978 1 78099 264 8

A CIP catalogue record for this book is available from the British Library.

Design: Stuart Davies

Printed in the USA by Edwards Brothers Malloy

We operate a distinctive and ethical publishing philosophy in all
areas of our business, from our global network of authors to
production and worldwide distribution.

CONTENTS

Foreword

by Caleb J. Ross

Phil Jourdan's rumination on the life and death of his mother will be easily dismissed by some readers as the product of an Oedipal urge, and to a degree the reader would be correct. But to forget the text entirely based on that single notion would be to forget the entire text. Jourdan himself acknowledges this danger:

> "The Freudian myth of a jealous, confused and perhaps parricidal infant strikes me as too narrow, too entrenched in the fascination of childhood to be of real use. In positing the infant's capacity for a much-too-zealous love of Mother, Freud condemned adult madness to a lesser order of import, the effect of an unsettled Oedipal anger."

This outright acknowledgement of a conflicted interest in the subject matter is exactly what makes Jourdan's style of narrative philosophy so appealing. We learn as Jourdan learns. We try out and apply various forms of thought to the subject as Phil tries out and applies these forms. Though the text places Jourdan's original interest in philosophy at age nineteen, I sense that he took to philosophy not as a byproduct of some intangible, fleeting interest but instead as conscious hunt for understanding as his own mother—which he knew not at the time but must have sensed somehow—fell into death.

Jourdan does not allow the constraints of perspective or chronology to guide the text. He comfortably slips into the perspective of other characters—from his mother, to the somewhat oppressive boarding school director, to his father, and more—easily and without warning, treating perspective as a fluid concept, not unlike the fluidity of thought itself. And though the author slips dangerously (read: engagingly) into hypothetical post-death interactions with the mother—often from her perspective—peeling back such scabs to delve into unresolution is the very idea around which *Praise of Motherhood* is built.

Though I cannot claim a relationship with my own mother to be one as simultaneously dynamic and nuanced as that which Jourdan and his own mother shared, I can claimed a mutual obsession with the subject matter of motherhood. I never had a present father (divorced when I was five), and like the author I've worked through and explored the role of a strong mother in my own writing. But what makes Jourdan's book so strong, and in turn so affecting, is that rather than exploring hypothetical fiction roles we understand every observation as a direct byproduct of a real-life mother-son dynamic.

Perhaps this book's great accomplishment is passing on the legacy of what the reader will come to know as a woman simply meant to exist beyond her own years. I found myself nodding along as she spoke, taking her words and Philippe's responses as a form of Socratic gospel, learning as Philippe learns, unearthing and revising my thought as Philippe did the same. In this way, Jourdan invites the reader to be a member of his family, literally extending his mother's impact to new generations and new lineages entirely.

Caleb J. Ross, author of *Stranger Will* and *I Didn't Mean to be Kevin*

To my sister, Mathilde, who knows the loss.
With thanks to the three people who read this book to death as it was being written: Michael Hulse, Irina Bortoi, and my father.
Thanks, as well, to my family: I owe them much of myself — in body, mind and joy.

Un lapin ne nous effraie point; mais le brusque départ d'un lapin inattendu peut nous mettre en fuite.
— Paul Valéry

ONE

It was Veterans Day; the Pope spoke into a microphone so the thousands around him could hear his weary voice. And in the airport lounge my sister and I waited for our flight to take off, trying not to listen to the televised broadcast of the Pope's solemn speech. I held my sister's hand and heard her say *fuck* for the first time.

"fuck, do you think she's going to be okay"

and I said "I don't know"

and she said "but why aren't they *telling* us what's going on"

"I don't know"

"I don't want mom to die"

"I know"

"I'm so scared"

"I know"

and the Pope went on, speaking of the dead, the men whose lives had been lost in a terrible war, and he praised them, their families, for the courage they'd shown. He spoke of Christ, but not much. Sometimes he closed his eyes and paused. From the airport lounge, sitting in front of the television screens, I had to rely on the cameras for a sense of what being there was like. Safe and comfortable and mourning out of patriotic or humanistic duty, in a spirit of contemplation. The Pope did not know that my mother was dying in a little hospital in Portugal. Neither did the lady who announced, on the intercom at the airport, that out of respect for the men who had lost their lives during the war however many decades ago now, we were all invited to stand for two minutes of silence. Everyone else in the lounge stood up, but my sister and I remained in our seats and hugged each other.

As far as I knew, my mother was dying or dead, a small, tanned Portuguese woman with curly dark hair and two dogs, two kids, a lovely loving wonderful lady, all of that sob-story

I

stuff. It turned out that when we were waiting for our flight, she was still alive. She would only die in the evening, after the Pope was done speaking and everyone was having dinner and no longer thinking about the veterans. But nobody had warned me. Nobody had warned anyone. Everybody was on the way to Portugal, my uncle, my grandfather, me and my sister, all of us trying to protect someone. They didn't tell me what had happened until I arrived in Portugal. I didn't tell my sister everything I knew, which was next to nothing, because I wanted to think I could protect her. I spoke to my father on the phone and he was in tears: "I will be there when you land," he said,

and I said:

"but why, what's going on"

"I'm not sure, I'm not sure, but if I were you... oh, Jesus, if I were you I would brace myself for the worst"

And he broke into tears and hung up. They had been separated fifteen years.

On the plane my sister and I spoke little. I told her it'd be okay. I told her even if the worst happened, I'd be around for her. You're my little sister. Tell me about Denver. How are classes going? She gave short, bored answers, and she asked me about my life. I told her I'd been about to take the train to Paris from London with a friend when I found out something was wrong with our mom.

"but what's *wrong* with her" my sister said

"I don't know"

"why don't they just *tell us*"

"because they're trying to keep us sane"

"how can I be sane when my mom is dying all of a sudden"

"I really don't know"

When we arrived in Portugal, and I saw my family standing together waiting for us — my grandparents, my father, my aunt — I knew at once there was no hope.

My mother had been taken to the big nothing and that was it

and what could I do about anything except to write and doodle and try my damnedest to cry — cry, for God's sake, cry, you ingrate, can't you even shed one tear for your mommy — nope, no crying, and that was a pretty recurrent problem for the next year or so, the lack of tears, the passionless way I dealt with everything — cry, if you don't cry you will never be taken seriously again — but by whom? Who cares if I cry, it won't change anything. And though I didn't cry I kept a series of notes, tiny memories it was important not to forget, ever-ever, things to stick into the book I had already decided to write about my mother.

I spent the night in my mother's house. When I got there, Vlad asked me how she was. I told him she was dead. And the world inside him seemed to collapse all at once, his muscular body trembled, he could not believe it, could not believe it, and he expressed himself in the best Portuguese he could. I could only understand half of what he was saying. Then he switched to Ukrainian and sobbed louder and hugged me and I was numb. The numbness lasted a year. You have lost the woman you wanted to marry, I wanted to say, and I have lost my mommy. We've probably lost the same thing.

I phoned my grandmother's house and spoke to my sister to see if she was all right:

"do you think you'll be okay tonight"

she said "yes"

"we'll see each other tomorrow"

"yes"

and there wasn't much to say apart from goodnight, I love you, things that were meaningless in the face of our non-mother. We hung up and I went into the kitchen to drink some water.

Mother was dead but there was still food in her fridge. What do you do with a dead woman's food? You don't eat it. That is like eating death itself. I gave it all to the dogs. All of it went splat on the floor and the dogs lapped it up. That was the first night.

She'd been dead three hours and already, like the selfish boy I was and am, I'd started removing little pieces of her from her own house. Letting the dogs eat everything in the fridge ought to have made them ill but they seemed fine. And anyway who cares if the dogs die. My mother was dead, and they were her dogs. Let them die with her. Let the dogs go back to that infinity like their precious mommy. I sat in that kitchen, marble tiles cold under my feet, open fridge humming, dogs slurping and chewing on everything from beans to raw beef to yogurt, and I felt a weird thickness in the brain that, I think, can only come when someone has died. You know the numbness: your shoulders are tense and your head is heavy, but it all feels natural. Loud thoughts about trivial things, a lot of pacing, clenched teeth, and the notion that you're teetering above some gaping abyss. It's a horrible thing to go through but there you have it. I started thinking about nothing in particular, certainly not about my mother, and I don't care if it's a defense mechanism, a way of dealing with the immediate pain of loss, but not thinking about your mother when she's just kicked the bucket is a pretty terrible thing to do, and I imagine everyone goes through it, so I'm not alone. I was alone that night, however. Me and the dogs, sitting around at the kitchen table, imagining a life without our mom, without pancakes in the morning, without intelligent discussions about things my sister found boring, without anything, for all I cared. The kitchen stank of food when I left it. I lay in bed for a while.

That repulsive image of my mother lying there in the hospital, brain-dead, breathing softly through tubes, nothing inside her head now except death. The machines were keeping her alive. God, make those machines work a little harder, don't just keep her alive for me to see this. I don't want to see it. Not the whistle-like breathing through tubes. This is not my mother, not as I want to remember her. If that's my mother then where is her smile, tell me that, and don't say she'll always be in my heart because she won't, she won't be anywhere that matters after she dies. She will be nowhere once she's not even here in the hospital bed. You show me where, exactly, my mother is in my heart. Which ventricle? How much blood does my mother require to linger in my heart? How do you show off how beautiful and wonderful your mother is when she's hidden in a muscle somewhere under your ribs? Where is her substance? What can your poetry do to make her less absolutely, terrifyingly, impossibly, absurdly dead?

I lay there and I thought of all this, wondered what I would do, tried to stop trying to make sense of the senseless. No good, of course, because we're terribly ambitious creatures when the time comes for new survival tactics. Oh, I will build a fire every day in your honor, mother, and it will keep me warm and it will provide me with the means to grill the deer that I'll have hunted during the day, and I will fall asleep by your light and wake up covered in ash. Stupid thoughts like that. Everything takes on a certain importance when you feel you've lost the biggest part of the world. You are forced to adjust your eyes and see the little things. Feel your way through the impalpable black.

I thought of the plane ride home, while everything was uncertain, before they'd told us what was going on. I'd held my sister's hand, looked out the window, blank-blank-blank mind and a weird tenseness in my muscles, let this be over soon, I don't care if she lives or dies as long as I don't have to guess the truth. They hadn't said, your mother is dying, they'd said get over here straight away and expect the worst and that was when I realized it was going to be bad, no simple operation, a major kind of thing. And quietly, on that plane journey, I resented each of them, resented them for not having told me before that my mother had fainted and been taken to a hospital where her life could end at any second. I'd tried to call her on the phone the day before and she hadn't answered so I tried again and no answer and soon I began to think something was wrong, but what do you do when something's wrong in Portugal and you're in England and all you have is a telephone? You call someone else, someone close to her, and that was her boyfriend, who spoke little Portuguese and no English, and in his rudimentary way he told me my mother had had an explosion in her brain, and I said what do you mean? An explosion in her brain, he said, I don't know what's going on, and I said where is she and he said the hospital and I said who's with her and he told me my grandmother was with her and nobody else was allowed in there. Heart pounding, sweating, all the symptoms, I tried to call my grandmother. No answer. So I called my grandfather and he said my mother's brain was being operated on, right now, he was flying in some doctor from New York and he would keep me posted, and he hadn't wanted to worry me by telling me earlier, and I wanted to say that it had only worried me even more but what can you do, everyone is a little different in dreadful circumstances.

But yes, I was lying in bed and thinking of all these things the night my mother died. One image in particular, one strange and terrible image, lingered above all in my head. The tubes were awful, and the beeping of the machines, and the brain-dead specimen on the bed, but the worst part was the nipple. When I arrived at the hospital they led me into the room where my mother was taking her last breaths. They left me alone there with my sister and my father, who'd come from another town to support us, the children, and to see his ex-wife one last time. I looked at that thing on the bed, like my mother but no longer *there*, no longer interested in me or my sister or anything else, simply a woman-shaped thing with tubes sticking in and out of it, in a little hospital gown that barely covered her, and I kissed her cheek without a tear and as I did so her arm fell from the bed and I saw my mother's nipple. The nipple from my infancy. So there it was. That nipple was her death. The instrument of my feeding was now the last sign of life within her. The breaths she took were artificial; her eyes were closed; there were no thoughts inside that shell of a head: but the nipple, which I was never supposed to see again, was uncovered and she felt no shame, no discomfort, not even mild embarrassment, because she was dead.

My grandmother walked into the room and we had a short debate on whether to ask a priest to come in and perform the last rites. She wanted none of it, but I said get the priest in here, even if you don't believe in God you should thank him because my mother felt no pain, or so you say, let's at least let the God we don't believe in have his holy way with my mother's soul, and I went on like that for a while, not quite sure what I was saying. So the priest came and talked to my mother for a while. Soon we were gone, in a daze, silent; my sister, in tears, went to my grandmother's house while my father drove me home. He had cried on the phone. I'd never heard him cry. On the way over to my house, I told my father it was okay, my mother lived on through me and I believed it and he did too but neither of us really believed it because she was kaput, she was nothing now. But we still believed it. It was also the first time in years I told my father I loved him. He did not say it back but he looked at me and said it with his eyes and that was enough for me.

And he said "yes you're right, we must help each other, you and I have more in common than most fathers and sons"

and I said "yes you're right, we do, drive me home and I'll come visit you soon..."

TWO

Why shouldn't the Oedipal situation happen much later than it was once fashionable to suppose? The Freudian myth of a jealous, confused and perhaps parricidal infant strikes me as too narrow, too entrenched in the fascination of childhood to be of real use. In positing the infant's capacity for a much-too-zealous love of Mother, Freud condemned adult madness to a lesser order of import, the effect of an unsettled Oedipal anger. Appealing as the idea of the issues of life stemming from the first hard years might be, I'm not convinced. Almost every criticism leveled at Freud that I've heard or read has seemed at least a bit convincing, but, in losing my mother and my own sense of purpose, I've grown most sensitive to what I believe is the fundamental problem of psychoanalysis's scientific pretensions: the assumption, noble-minded but deluded, that there is little of the mystical in one's love of one's mother. That is, the curious insistence of Reason in the face of something too murky and magical to be conquered by rational observation and medical dexterity. To put it simply: I loved my mother because she was a terrible beauty, because she was my Mommy, because she was Love manifest. It was a religious, feverish thing, irreducible to the jargon of the expert therapist. We are all amateurs in this regard: just as even the most erudite scholar knows nothing of eternity and cowers before the most basic questions, the therapist trained in psychoanalysis is as powerless in his relation to the mother-god as his patient is. Everyone, even in his profoundest hatred, loves his mother.

The taboo of the child enamored of his parent is easy to misunderstand. The vulgarity of treating love as a purely sexual thing should be dismissed immediately. To be in love with your mother does not have to mean what common parlance would have it mean. When she died, I tried to think up things about my mother that I found repulsive: there was little. Perhaps, then, I had idealized her to such an extent that I was, in the literal sense, in love with her. There's no shame in this. It is not a question of erections and love letters. It is about mad, uncritical, unashamed loyalty to an object elevated to the status of perfection. Of course she was flawed: my mother made extremely human mistakes, performed all the rituals of the mortal, engaged in the pleasures of the earth and was occasionally too cowardly to do the right thing. But in spite of every imperfection she may have possessed, I cannot fault her for a single thing, and that is why, in my religious insanity, I place her above the idea of God the Father.

Strangely, it was of these things that I thought during the funeral. While the priest droned on in Portuguese and my sister cried and my grandfather cried and everyone else stood in silence, I was thinking of the Freudian question. The train of thought seemed to go in a very particular, predetermined fashion, as though everything else were an illusion and what mattered was that I should arrive at the disturbing truth that I had lost the one thing I had treasured above all else. Though I could see the mourning people around me, in tears and in black, and though I wasn't blind to the gravity of the moment, even the realization of my loss felt rather like an abstract, intellectual game, nothing solid, an experiment in thought from which I would soon wake to find my mother sitting by my side, happy, unharmed. Hugging my sister, whispering that we'd be okay, still I was not entirely there, and my consciousness was aimed at the crucial problem of psychoanalysis, something in which I'd held an especial interest for the previous three years. If I agree with anything Freud said, it is that the psychological, perhaps uncontrollable defense mechanism is a huge force in our dealings with the terror of events. Nothing seemed more important than the mystery of the unconscious at that moment, and so, ignoring the darkness of the present, I retreated into a stupor of irrelevant thoughts. My central concern was the exact point at which, in my greatest youth, I'd considered my father a danger and resolved in my clumsy way to protect my mother-related interests. Though I am certain a Freudian would find a way to explain it, I could not accept the basic premise: my father had been far too absent in my first few years for me to feel threatened; nor did I bear him grudge anymore, if I ever had. I had, to all purposes, been a mommy's boy, an overprotected, spoilt, capricious and difficult child, and my father had simply not entered into the equation until my teens. Had I, then, failed to be imprinted with a suitable level of respect for authority? Did I unconsciously believe that the Freudian hypothesis was an affront to my conception of self?

It was not until the priest asked us to join him in prayer that I managed to step out of these musings. I did not know the words to the prayer. All my life I had fought a battle against speaking Portuguese, likening it to a cyst in my brain, a tongue unfit for my mouth. I considered it a blessing to have learned to speak English, my means of interacting with the greater part of those I met. Now it was the Portuguese language through which everyone was expected to say goodbye to my mother. The routine seemed stupid to me, but there was nothing to be done, so I pretended to mumble something when the others did. Little by little, as the prayer went on, I slipped back into a reverie. This time it wasn't Freud, but Auschwitz. Cheer up, I told myself. You could be in a camp. Six million Jews died and they didn't get the luxury of an organized funeral. Six million Jews; that's far more than all the words in the three languages you speak. Six million Jews; more than all the people you have ever known, and all the people that they have ever known. You are unlucky to have lost your mother, but you are lucky to have lost her here, now, like this. An aneurysm is better than the gas chamber. A funeral is better than being turned into soap. Is that legend true? Were they really made into soap? So many myths surrounding those years... so many myths that some lunatics go as far as to claim it's all a myth. Should I write a novel in which it is proven that the

Holocaust *was* a myth? As a thought experiment: a Jewish scholar finds evidence of a widespread conspiracy. The Holocaust never happened... but he can't accept it, he needs proof. He spends the first hundred pages looking for this proof. He finds it. What a dilemma. Should he go forth with the discovery and expose the myth of the extermination of six million Jews? Keep quiet? Should the truth be told here? If I were a Jew, would I have a different conception of death now that the Shoah has happened?

By the time I'd snapped out of my thoughts again there was nothing to see except a coffin being lowered into the earth. Nothing special. I was too absorbed in the orgasm of abstract thought to appreciate fully how dangerously close to death my body was at that moment. Not my own death, not yet, but the death of a body from which my own had bloomed. Once the coffin was in the ground, some bored-looking men started to slide the dirt over it. The process seemed never to end, so I looked around. A woman I didn't know was standing far from me, behind a cousin of mine, a woman of such incredible, angelic beauty, with earth-colored hair and black eyes, that I instantly forgot where I was. The effect of her beauty was such that, despite the heavy sunlight, I found it impossible not to keep my eyes wide open and stare at her face. The serenity in her gaze unsettled me. It was the look of someone too beautiful to be a screen actress, too wise to impart wisdom and too powerful to address directly. I had no notion of who she might be, nor did I care. It was perhaps the first time I'd ever beheld someone so beautiful without the pangs of lust: there was nothing in me but a sense of timid awe. At that moment, with the sun behind her casting a shadow the tip of which just missed touching my mother's grave, I wondered if I might be hallucinating. Nothing that happened afterwards helped to dispel the thought: the woman did not attend the lunch after the funeral, and nobody made mention of her. A variety of explanations presented itself:

she was someone's wife; she was an old friend of my mother's; she was the perfection of my mother's soul given human form. It didn't matter: when everything was over, when I was alone in my room and everyone who wasn't family had left, the only important fact was that something beyond intellectual self-indulgence had kept me alive through the burial. It was a rare moment in which I could tell myself, without the faintest trace of irony or cynicism, that beauty had saved me.

THREE

Childhood was normal: pets, misunderstandings, temper tantrums, candy, the constant worry that things — the house, the family, the living conditions — were insufficient and that we'd turn out weird, or worse, unhappy. It was a normal childhood to the extent that everyone (the maids, my sister and I, the old seamstress who came once a week and spent her time chattering about her nieces) — everyone panicked about not being normal enough. Everyone except my mother, who long before had stopped caring about the normal state of things, the myth of normality, the dream of conformity. The pets and the candy cravings and the temper tantrums were things she accepted and dealt with. Everything was fine because she didn't strive to make us conveniently compliant. She let us sulk after our tantrums, work through the misunderstandings. She sighed a great deal and cleaned up a good deal more and every day told us she loved us. Through those superhuman efforts, she made us the only normal family around.

We — my sister and I, the dogs, the cats and hamsters — all conspired to make the house a mess. I used to burn things. My sister scribbled things on the antique furniture. The dogs shat in shoes and the cats scratched at one of the couches. The hamsters escaped from their cages and nibbled their way into the yellow flowery curtains. And there were chinchillas in cages always kicking sand around, birds spitting out seeds, fish forever dying. Hard work. Our mother hired a series of maids. I can't remember the order — did the helpless tiny confused Filipino woman come before or after the squinting fat woman who helped herself to everything in the fridge and then denied the deed? What was the name of the one who brought men into the house when we weren't there? It was a procession of unfit candidates. By the time my mother settled on a kind grey-haired woman who forgot to do everything she was instructed to do, I was no longer interested in the various weirdoes walking in and out of the house. I was comfortable, and I made messes everywhere. Only the kind old woman with the memory problems was patient (or forgetful) enough to deal with my chaos.

Before the problems began, before I asked my mother to let me attend boarding school, my mother and I seemed to strike an unspoken agreement. As long as I didn't tease my sister too much, and as long as my grades were good, I was allowed to be a little grinning bastard all day long. I destroyed all my toys with hammers and matches. Plastic soldiers, toy cars, my sister's dolls. Everything fun for a while, then fascinating in flames. Burn everything, all the old junk I didn't want anymore. Step out on the terrace and set fire to it all. And my mother never raising her voice, but sounding sad and amused at the same time, saying:

"what are you doing this time"

"I'm burning Action Man"

"why"

"because I'm bored"

And I wasn't even bored; I simply wanted to make her voice shrill. I never succeeded. She'd take the matches from my hand and toss them in the trash and call the maid and send me to my room. And I'd refuse, so she'd say it again and I'd refuse, and eventually I'd feel guilty and walk to my room and sulk. That was our relationship in those early years: I pushed and pushed and she moved aside and let me fall. Then she helped me up again and told me she loved me. I told her I loved her. A few hours later I'd be destroying another toy.

She was a single mother living in a large duplex apartment in the middle of Lisbon with two kids and too many animals. Everyone and everything was a handful. She had no reason to work as a professor at a local university. She didn't need the money — her father's generosity allowed us to live comfortably. I think she worked because she didn't want to feel idle. She didn't want to think her whole life was one mess to clean up after another. When she'd walked us to school and given the maid enough instructions for the maid to be sure to forget, my mother drove to work and taught computer programming and mathematics in a hot airless room to students she never spoke about at home. Work was her escape, her way of feeling useful beyond the confines of home. She worked, not to ward off material poverty, but to fight the anemia of routine and loneliness.

She worked because when my sister and I were at school, and the maid was scrubbing the floor, and the seamstress, who came several times a week because my mother took pity on her — the wrinkled spinster-seamstress was lonelier than the rest of us combined, a woman spurned by her only love decades earlier and only now accepting she'd never find someone else — and while the pets were quietly sleeping in the sunlight creeping in through the blinds, and the television was finally off, and the sounds of perennial traffic had blurred into a numbing humming of noise she could barely hear — she was engulfed by every kind of solitude. No boyfriend back then; the children disapproved of anyone she brought home, as a matter of principle, or envy. (But Mommy, if you have a new boyfriend then you'll never be with Daddy again) — No close friends; such was the trust she inspired in people, her aura of wisdom, that almost anyone she spoke to grew to depend on her for emotional support: it was near impossible for my mother to unburden herself on those who treated her like a therapist. (I'm sorry to call you this late and I'm sorry I've been so, uh, out of touch but you won't believe what's happened and I need your help, Sophia) — And no real hobbies anymore: she tried cooking but found it exhausting after we learned to take her cooking for granted; she tried amateur astronomy, learning the shapes of constellations and pointing them out at night before our bedtime, but that could only happen at the close of ever more tiring days. So our mother was lonely, and the best way she knew to break the fingers of strangling solitude was work. She was qualified to teach — so she taught.

She took me with her to class one day. I was twelve, shy, not interested in much. I hadn't wanted to go with her, and I can't remember why she had to take me. She sat me down at the back of the auditorium (so different from the classrooms I was used to, so much bigger, so barren-looking) and told me to keep really quiet: "it'll only be an hour, after that I'll take you back home"

"but I don't wanna be here at *all*"

"well, kiddo, we don't have much of a choice, anyway, when I'm finished teaching I'll show you the computers"

"can I play on them"

"there aren't any games on these computers"

"then I don't want to"

"just one hour, I promise"

"why don't the computers have games"

"because these students are here to learn how to program other things"

"I want to be a computer programmer"

"then you should sit still and pay attention"

She was a soothing speaker, a timid teacher. She didn't raise her voice, but she kept it just loud enough that everyone could hear. No hand movements, a bit of pacing. Her students didn't seem to care, but they didn't seem bored either. Nobody passed notes around, and it was not quite yet the age of ubiquitous cell phones. Except for my mother's voice and the sounds of keyboards being typed on, there was nothing to listen to. I heard her voice in a new way, almost authoritative, explaining things that made no sense to me, using words I'd never heard, and she seemed like an impostor: not my mother who sent me to bed or asked if I would please walk the dog for her just this one time or asked what the hell I was burning now, but a lady who looked like my mother and whose voice had that same sad milky quality yet said things that were alien in every way. The students all around looked at her and saw the only version of my mother they knew, a humble teacher who marked their papers leniently and used words like *Boolean* and *integer* instead of *I love you, kiddo*. They didn't know her. They weren't privy to her real beauty. And still they had a grownup access to her public face that I simply didn't see often enough for that face to seem familiar. They asked questions impersonally and she answered impersonally and at those moments, when she was transmitting information instead of showing love, I was overwhelmed with curiosity, sadness, a sense of not knowing her as well as I wanted to.

By this point I was shifting with discomfort in my seat. Seeing my mother transformed into a weirdly familiar stranger had agitated me so much that I needed to move, to crack my knuckles or kick at the air a little bit to loosen my leg muscles. But I couldn't. I had promised to be quiet and it felt wrong to break a promise made to that lady at the blackboard with my-motherly qualities. So I remained seated and moved my toes as subtly as I could to avoid letting them rub against the soles of my shoes — somehow the idea that rubbing the soles could produce a sound had entered my thoughts and it seemed better not to tempt fate. I squirmed and wriggled like a tortured worm but nobody noticed. I was sitting farther from the front of the class than anyone else. Nobody could see me. And so my squirming grew livelier. I didn't know what I was doing — but I needed to move and I moved, pinching my skin and scratching my armpits, running my fingers over my forehead and feeling for sweat. It was hot. There was a dead insect on my table.

I had not noticed the insect before. I stopped moving and lowered my head forwards to inspect it. The bug had wings but didn't look like any fly I'd ever seen. Its body seemed greenish one moment and black-blue the next. It was lying near the upper right corner of my desk. My head was so close to its corpse that my breathing made its wings and legs quiver. But the bulk of the corpse itself didn't move. Something was holding it in place. Reaching over the table with my little arm I touched the thick

whitish substance under the insect's body and, at once understanding, recoiled. Chewing gum. Someone wiser and more
mature than me had captured the tiny winged monster and
pushed it into a wad of chewing gum on the table and left it to
die. How long had it suffered? How long ago? I examined the
body again. A truly ugly creature. A furry-legged twitching thing
lying supine on a bed of gum. And the questions kept arising.
Who had done this? How had they captured the insect without
attracting the attention of the class? How had they managed to
press an insect into discarded chewing gum without crushing the
insect's tiny legs into powder? Had the gum already been there,
or had the perpetrator decided to chew the gum on purpose to
use it as a torture instrument once its flavor had vanished?

The world around me lost its realness and I looked only at the
gum and the bug. I couldn't hear my mother's voice any longer,
couldn't hear the students clearing their throats and the click-
clicking of typing. Everything became the dead bug. The longer I
stared at it, the less threatening it seemed — yet as soon as I
blinked its monstrousness was restored, it seemed new and gross
again, the disgust welled up in me and I thought: this is the most
terrifying thing in the world. And I'd stare at it some more, at its
twitchy legs and implausible eyes and again I'd grow used to it.
Then I'd blink and once more I was shaking with revulsion. Who
knows how long this went on for? But it seemed eternal,
punishment for who knew what misdeed. Staring at that insignif-
icant loss of life, an insect nobody in the world knew was dead or
had ever existed, an insect even its murderer would probably
have forgotten by now, I could do nothing but feel sorry for it, or
for myself. My identity was merging with that of the bug. We
were caught in gum.

Class ended and my mother walked over to me very slowly,
wearing some kind of concern or curiosity on her face, saying:

"what's wrong, kiddo"

and she sat at the table next to mine and I pointed at the insect.

She made a face and said:

"did you do that"

"no, of course not"

"the poor thing, it must have been attracted to the sugar in the gum and got stuck there"

"no, someone put it in there"

"how do you know that"

"I'm sure someone did"

"well, we should clean it up before the next class"

"why"

"because that would be courteous"

"I don't want to touch it"

"you don't have to, let me do it"

She took out a tissue from her handbag and used it to pinch the gummy carcass and pull it away from the table, and threw the tissue in a nearby trashcan.

"there"

But something was wrong inside me. She sensed it.

"What's wrong"

"I feel strange"

"what is it"

"I don't know what it is, I feel strange"

"well, come on, I'll take you home, thank you for being so patient"

"I feel really weird"

"do you have a headache"

"no"

"stomach ache"

"no"

"okay, come on"

and she helped me up and drove me home.

Childhood was normal because, though I was too sensitive to function the way my classmates did, the way the neighbors' children behaved, my mother treated me like the only normal kid she'd ever met. It was a year or so before she died that she told me, over a meal of roast beef she could barely handle because she hadn't eaten meat in so long (but it's good for your anemia — yes, I know, but that doesn't mean it's easy to eat), that she had always had a secret fear. She feared losing me to my oversensitivity. She was so thankful to have seen me grow into someone more mature and functional and nearly happy with himself than I had promised to be — the boy who couldn't take seeing a dead fly was becoming a strong young man, and she was proud of that. You used to get me so worried. When your first hamster died, you were so shocked that I had to call the doctor because you were shaking so much. Do you remember that? You were nine or ten. You saw your hamster lying cold and dead in its cage and you got hysterical, you wouldn't listen to me and wouldn't calm down and all day you broke things and shook and sobbed. By the time I'd called the doctor and set up an appointment you had a fever. That was the first time I wondered if everything was all right with you. Psychologically. I was worried. And I was right to worry — because I have always loved you far more than you suspected. That day when you saw the fly glued to the table with gum was frightening for me. You went very quiet. And I kept thinking, what has he seen that was so traumatic? Why does he care so much about a fly? But of course I knew why. Because you were like me. When I was young, I befriended every creature I encountered. I went swimming in the lake and frogs followed me. Did I ever tell you that story? I have a friend named Natalie and she was a frog. She followed me around for an hour while I was in that lake in France. I was a child and it was enchanting. Then she grew bored and left and I began to cry. And that's what you were like, as well. You cared too much about trivial things. Like the cruelty of rubbing a fly into a bit of old gum. That was too much for you. So you cried and I kept wondering if this was normal for a twelve- year-old boy. Was it normal? But I didn't have an answer and soon your sobs stopped and I understood that it didn't matter if you were normal or not, it was a false distinction in the first place, you didn't need to be anything other than happy. I was proud of having a child whose conscience was a little too strong, instead of the other way round. I always wanted a good son and even if you were perhaps too focused on being good when you weren't being a little pest, that was exactly right and I felt proud. But seeing you crying like that, the day I took you to my class, I had to wonder if there was something inside you that I couldn't see, couldn't reach and keep close. You were my son but a stranger's son, too. You seemed so different from your usual grumpy, friendly self. You were just shattered.

And she held me as I sobbed, upset about far more than a dead insect but incapable of expressing anything to myself or to her. Was it the insect I was crying about, or had that moment simply served as catalyst for the change? Did I even care about it anymore? I was crying. There was nothing but sadness for the sake of sadness in my tears, and I, ill-equipped to deal with pure incommunicable sadness (not misery and not hatred, just sadness), learning only now of the senselessness of mourning for things that had never mattered yet took on the proportions of mountains when focused on too long, could only keep crying. My mother held me. I was so worried about you, kiddo. You seemed too upset; I suspected you were hiding something from me. Maybe someone had hurt you. I asked you and you couldn't reply, and you breathed, and you said no, no, no, I don't know why I'm crying so much. So I just held you.

FOUR

Had my mother been a sterner, angrier, perhaps a darker-spirited woman, she might have said the following when I first told her that I'd gone to see a doctor on my own, a doctor who might be able to cure me, to find a way to stop the hopelessness that characterized my adolescence:

"You do not believe in angels, nor can you, because you don't believe in God; so you believe in nothing, you are aimless, trapped in a big void, you think you're free to do as you please because there is no ground beneath your feet and no sky above you, there is no *something beyond*, there's no way for things to mean. You find yourself despondent at the best moments because you can't allow yourself to share in the joys of the righteous. To you there's no such thing. And how could it be otherwise? Consistently you've disobeyed me, and that is bad enough; but you've refused to listen when I speak, not from my own wisdom, but from the position of someone who accepts Christ. You don't know Christ, and you don't know anything besides. Yet I won't force you to be saved. No rituals will help you unless you want to be helped. There is no Pascalian routine to follow in this house before you can believe. You accept God or you do not, there's no middle ground, and if you think there is, you are even more deluded than you seem. What do you need your doctor for? What bone have you broken?"

Had she been made of such stuff, my mother could have said all this a hundred times throughout my teenage years. She could have taken me to the priests in France of whom she was so fond, sat me down in front of them and said: Talk to this boy. Talk to him and make him see. And if they were really as wise as my mother claimed, they'd have looked at me and then looked at her, and said:

"There's nothing to be done. Look at him: He lusts after his classmates and writes stories filled with anger and hatred. He despises the weak though he is weak himself. Look at him closely, stupid woman, and see his acne, his pallor, and his fierceness. He's not looking for salvation, nor should he be. He'd make a terrible convert, because he has all the attributes of a Christian already, a typical Catholic. You say he feels guilty at the slightest thing, that he crumbles under the weight of guilt thanks to nothing at all. Let him! What does he need us for, if he is already so morbid? Why should we tarnish his perfect conscience when he already has so much of it, and so much to be ashamed of? He doesn't need to be converted. Don't let Catholic practices ruin him when he's already such a perfect believer."

Such a conversation would have crushed me. To the uncertainties of adolescence it is better not to add the burden of a god. Though I never had to worry about my soul's salvation in my mother's company, it wasn't difficult to detect, in some capacity, certain signs that my mother was a believer. Yet I know very little of my mother's religious attitude.

A few things are certain. She had no doubt of God's existence, but this was a God who dwelled in every rock and every tree and waterfall, a God of Things as well as persons, one as fascinated by the animals we eat as by the people we convert to our cause. When she spoke of God she spoke of him informally, with none of the haughty piety of the ardent believer, no trace of the atheist's exasperation. She did not need to speak of such things very often. God almost never entered her discourse, and if he did, after you pressed her, she was casual about it, as if we all already knew that God is not only in us all but in all the animals and all the demons. A beacon of pantheism. She saw in dogs the very same substance we proclaim ours alone. When she banged her head against a shelf, or let the knife slip and cut her finger, she got angry at nobody: who could she blame but herself, and why should she blame herself when there was nothing to be angry about? She accepted her place in the world because the world was hers, the world was everything and something more.

God in all things, and all things in God, and a quiet resolution never to grow too furious about much. I have no doubt that, when I was first diagnosed with the depression that would later bloom into psychosis, she sought religious counsel; but the priests she spoke to must have been very unorthodox, at least as sacrilegious as she was, perhaps even more so, driven to insanity as they ought to have been by celibacy and open-mindedness. Perhaps she telephoned the priest whose name I have forgotten, the priest in France of whom she spoke very fondly: a little man, she said, no taller than a young girl, but wise and kind. Not the type to bring God into conversation at all, not a man interested in recruiting into the Army of Light.

This priest died about two years before my mother. Because I didn't live with her, I had made it a habit of dutifully calling her several times a week. On the day she heard that her favorite priest, let us call him Father X, had died, she picked up the phone in a voice a little too husky to seem hers. She said hello, my child. What's wrong, I said, and she said an old friend of mine died yesterday and I am very sad, it is a sad thing but he was old, he must have been in his nineties, but I'm very sad.

That is how she expressed herself even on a good day, with repetitions and a mellow voice that she almost never raised, so when she was sad the effect was strange. Just as we expect a happy dog never to stop wagging its tail, I had come to believe my mother's joy was inexhaustible. Yet I was as capable as anyone of being selfish on the worst of occasions, and on that day I was hardly willing to listen, really to listen, to my mother's aggrieved voice. I had things to say to *her*. I had a lesson in ten minutes. She could talk to me about this later. I'm sorry to hear it, I said, and tried to find a delicate way to change the subject. She didn't press on, and soon I'd forgotten all about the death of a priest of whom I had heard wonderful things but who meant nothing to me. Now, guilt-ridden and wearing my writer's hat, I can only imagine the rest. I suppose she put down the phone after I was done ranting and began to sob very gently. She made herself decaffeinated coffee, sat at the kitchen table and spoke aloud to the cat. But what she said, on the surface, had nothing to do with the dead priest. Hello, my beautiful kitty. You're beautiful. Oh, who's purring? Who's purring like a little princess… Inside the fires raged, she could not accept her lot, the death of a man she had respected and looked up to. Death is not a cruel fate but it is sad and lonesome. Perhaps, she thought, I will manage to speak about Father X with Philippe someday. He's probably not interested in things like that. But he will be when he realizes how much I loved Father X. When my friends and I went camping in France, and we first met him, I think I even fell in love with him. But that was so long ago.

Her thoughts must have been a mix of Portuguese, Russian, French and English, all languages in which she was fluent. She had told me, once, that she wasn't even sure what language it was she had most of her thoughts in. This baffled me. I could only think in English after years of speaking it at home and at school. My mother, however, made no choice between them, and I have the impression she simply switched from one to the other arbitrarily. Or perhaps she thought in English when she dealt with me, in Portuguese when she spoke to her parents, Russian with her boyfriend, and French when she remembered her beloved Father X. "Quel dommage," he might have said if he'd been able to know she was dead. What a shame. That's all I can picture him saying, from the way she described him. A man resigned to his mortality, to the death of everyone he knew, to the complete extinction of life, but also a man able to enjoy himself and comfort others because of this acceptance. He was someone whose priority was not God but Love, and so a heretic. No doubt he was fluent in other languages, as well. When they conversed, they may have gone from French to English without noticing it. Masters of many tongues. Now that they are both gone it feels as though each of their languages were missing a few words.

The last time she spoke to Father X was when I was fourteen. That was also the first time I ever heard of him. In my adolescent despair I had caused despair in my mother, too, and she felt unable to cope without speaking to someone whom she considered to be on her level. I know very little of the conversation she had with him. They hadn't spoken in years, so the first ten minutes must have been warm and full of pleasant reminiscences. But she had called him for something specific. She needed guidance from a man whose priority was not to preach but to listen. Such a man does not exist everywhere. So when she finally got around to telling him what she was going through, I have no doubt that he listened carefully, without a single interruption.

She (probably) said:

"I have two children. My son is fourteen, and my daughter is twelve. It's my son that I'm worried about. His name is Philippe. For about a year, now, he's been growing angrier by the day, really angry, a violent, terribly sad kind of anger that doesn't allow room for other people's sympathy. I don't know what to do with him. I think he doesn't even know I love him. He screams, he throws things, and he moans about feeling horrible. Whenever I try to speak to him about it, he begins to cry. I'm afraid of him, I fear he could do something stupid."

Father X told her to carry on, and so she did. She told him Philippe had always been complicated, naïve, arrogant, insecure, good-natured but confused, the sort of boy not to make friends very easily. Now he was in a boarding school in Switzerland, an expensive place, a school with fewer than two hundred students, in the mountains, where everyone did a lot of sports, with nice food, friendly teachers; but even so Philippe was unhappy. He had gone to see a doctor on his own because he was convinced nobody would ever take him seriously otherwise. The doctor had given him antidepressants. The pills were causing Philippe to put on weight. The weight was making Philippe unhappy, as were the people around him, his own insecurities, the weight of existence itself and, perhaps, his mother. Oh, what if she was part of the problem? What if she wasn't good enough, or strong enough, to handle him? Was that why he resented her, why he shouted at her sometimes? Was that why he had stopped telling her things?

She worried about him every day, but never more so than now. He had just been in hospital. This was it, she hoped: the culmination, the crisis, the very worst part of the whole ordeal. Now he had been kept asleep for a few days while they'd had him on an IV drip to give him certain substances she didn't know much about but that the doctors had seriously recommended, now he was feeling a little more awake, she thought she could try to talk to him, to plan for the future. He'd had a crisis but it was nothing to get worked up about anymore, right? She could handle this. If he screamed at her, so be it, but she'd be damned before she gave up on her son. Why had he been in hospital? Because there was no other way. He'd had a collapse, some sort of episode, a breakdown of the mind, she didn't really know, or she didn't understand. It had started during the summer, when the family was on a cruise ship, and it had ended in hospital, and the whole thing was very complicated and she had managed to grasp none of it. He'd told her he was feeling paranoid. People were watching him, talking, plotting against him, they wanted to hurt him, and he was trapped on the ship with nowhere to go somewhere on the Adriatic coast. What was she supposed to do, as a mother, when he would not even listen to her as a human being? When she told him nobody was out to hurt him, no one was even looking at him when they ate in the restaurant, surrounded by a hundred other people, he dismissed her words as part of the conspiracy.

"They are looking at me," he said. "They make fun, and they want me to suffer. They're looking because they know what I've done."

And what had he done? Nothing. He was innocent of all serious sins, and he insisted on this when she pressed him, but when he spoke of those watching him, he hinted at something else, a deeper kind of guilt, and they knew, the people around him saw not only what he had done, but what he, in his capacity as a thinking and acting human, *could yet do*, and that was enough to set him quivering and muttering something about the conspiracy on the ship. When he looked over his shoulder and locked eyes with someone, a chattering woman or a man sitting alone drinking his beer, he assumed, unquestioningly, that those eyes represented all of mankind's vision and maybe things beyond. Who is watching me, he said, who is it trying to do things? Everyone. He would leave the dinner table abruptly and rush back to his cabin as discreetly as he could, ignoring his mother's pleas for him to remain. He'd sit in the cabin and dig his fingernails into his forehead and say why is this happening, what's going on... but soon the paranoia would not allow such interrogation, the point was not the Why but the When and How will they get me, what do they want to do to me? Why does my sweat smell of blood? Why does the cabin smell of something strange, like onions, this cabin stinks of onions.

The smell of the onions, a smell only he could detect, was the first true hallucination. There had been little things, things no longer worth mentioning, that he believed he'd seen or heard or smelled during the cruise, but the overpowering reek of onions was the first Big Problem. Onions that should not be in the cabin were giving off a horrible stench everywhere inside the cabin, from the bed to the toilet sink. Yet there were no onions, none that he could see, and this made him furious, there had to be onions somewhere, and he would find them. He tore the pillows open, threw everything he could onto the floor, kicked the table around, looking for those forsaken onions, he'd find them, he'd prove he wasn't insane...

Father X may have been scratching his chin as he heard my mother tell him these things about Philippe. Sophia, he said to my mother, you have had a very difficult time. But she went on, she told him how Philippe had asked her if she could smell the onions, and she had said she couldn't, so he'd begun to scream, saying you have to, you must smell it, I do, why can't you? And the most unsettling thing was that he was convinced she was lying to him, that it was some practical joke or worse, and she was in on it, trying to humiliate him or torture him for the amusement of the guests.

When the ship stopped for a day in St Petersburg, and the sky was overcast but bright, everything seemed normal again. The onion incident had left the cabin in a mess, but after that Philippe's behavior was irreproachable. He joined the family for dinner once in a while and went for jogs around the ship, took in the salty air, stared at waves, read books, laughed. Sometimes he told jokes. They discussed his latest writing project. He'd written a short novel before, but this time he wanted to create something enormous, a way to show the world what was inside him. She listened to his rambling descriptions of every character, place and emotion that he hoped to stick into his novel. The tensions between the protagonist, who was clearly based on Philippe himself, and the world around him... the possible titles for each chapter, some pretentious, some clever, most juvenile... She didn't mind sitting in the sun on the deck listening and saying nothing discouraging, because she was proud, and because she was worried. Talk of novel writing was interesting, but she knew that at any moment he could lose his grip on reality.

St Petersburg brought it on. They joined a tour group and visited churches, parks, a little restaurant. Gulls flapped around overhead, people glared at other people, cars nearly collided but never honked: there was an eerie muteness to the city, and when they found themselves in an enormous cathedral the monks' singing came as if out of a different world. Those baritone voices, those grotesque depths of mortal song before God, caused Sophia to stop listening to her tour guide and instead focus on a certain infinity she could only tap into when the moment was bleak, as it had been for days. What would happen to her son? What was going on inside that head of his? She gave herself up to the song, lowered her gaze, mused on the horror of the previous week, wondered where everything was headed. The monks were singing in Russian, and she understood, but she did not care about the words, or even the melody, but only what the singing represented; submission to a thing so frightening it could only destroy. Her view on the matter of God, for so long a pleasant one, was shattered. God was a frightening, demanding, destructive thing if the fate of her son was any evidence. There was no room in the universe for goodness. Even if she took perfect care of Philippe she would be repaid in a few moments of bliss amid many years of hardship. She would never know what would become of him after her death. These thoughts, which she'd dismissed so often as irrelevant to the great parental task, now took on a gravity she couldn't handle. Why bother?

Why, indeed? But a nudge brought her back.

"Look over there" and he pointed to a crowd of people walking into the cathedral.

She said

"what is it"

and he pointed again and said

"look at that man, the fat one, the one in a green shirt, do you see him" "no"

"damn it" he said "he's right there"

and he pointed a third time and said

"can't you see him?"

"no"

"but he's there and he's been everywhere we've been, he's following us, why is he following us"

"he isn't"

"he is"

"show me exactly who you mean"

and Philippe described a man who simply was not there. No man in the crowd seemed as fat, as bearded, as grotesquely evil as Philippe claimed. The more she looked, the less she paid attention. Someone in her head was screaming, announcing the news, it was all going downhill again, he was sinking away.

"Kiddo" she said "there's no such person there, do you want to go home"

He shook his head and said

"he *is* there, he's there, you bitch, why do you have to lie to me"

Sophia's hand was on his shoulder now.

"let's go"

"no"

"why not"

"as long as they keep singing, we're okay"

"who"

"the monks"

"why"

but he didn't answer.

She noticed, then, the torrents of sweat falling off his forehead, and she said

"let's go, let's get you to bed"

"no, no, no"

"please, kiddo"

"no, he's standing in the way, how the fuck are we supposed to get out of here"

What was he imagining? How could she tell him that nobody was in the way, when, in his private world, the kid was convinced of the man's existence, of the man's utter malice? To make sure it wasn't all some terrible mistake, she looked again, but there were only five or six elderly women being led by a young man, another tour guide, around the cathedral. No trace of the fat, evil, elusive presence that so disturbed her son. So she stood and she took his hand, then she looked at her daughter who had been sitting silently by her side, and she took her daughter's hand and led her children out of the cathedral, whispering to Philippe not to look at the fat man. Too conscious of being watched, Philippe didn't reply, fixed his gaze on his feet, they walked away, towards the dock, to the cabin.

Father X, at this point in Sophia's narrative, was sitting down, scrawling a picture on a pad of paper next to the phone. He could hear her words but he needn't listen any longer. He'd reached that moment in any sustained act of *listening* where even without paying attention to the words, one knows exactly what another is saying. All of these details, these ugly things, the tragedy of Sophia's life, were superfluous to him, but essential to her; for while she believed that only by recounting events exactly as they had occurred would her story make any sense to him, he was perfectly aware of the situation already. It was in her voice, her intonations. If she needed to vent, let her, by all means; but it would not change the advice he would give her at the end.

He snapped back to attention when he realized she was saying something about Philippe deciding to jump off the deck of the ship and into the sea. Some crisis, a new variation on the curse, had come about, and after banging his head on the walls so hard that he'd almost lost consciousness, the boy, in a fit of hatred toward his mother, had shoved her onto the floor and said

"you stay the fuck away from me, don't you touch me"

32

and he'd started walking towards the deck, saying

"I am going to die, I am going to die for fuck's sake, you worthless bitch"

and she'd pushed herself off the floor and had run after him. It was night. There was no storm. The waves were gentle.

She managed to grab his arm and she pleaded. He was in tears but she was not. All the goodness and warmth in her was gone, replaced by a cold, deliberate awareness that may not have been hers, and she said

"stay there"

and she sat him on the stairs. They sat in silence. He could barely see his mother in her now, as though his raging and bullying had turned her into a cracked shell. Her eyes looked tired. She was void of life, and the void beckoned. He watched. She didn't move, nor did she appear to breathe, and soon he wiped the tears off of his face and said

"are you okay"

"yes, I'm all right, let's get you to bed"

Without fussing he followed her back to the cabin and he got into bed. She sat by his side and didn't say a word and waited until he fell asleep. Then she got into her own bed and, trying not to wake her daughter, she cried the only way she could cry: very gently, very peacefully.

The next day the ship's doctor came and gave Philippe some medicine. It put the kid to sleep. "I recommend you take him to a clinic," the doctor said, "so you can figure out what's best for him with proper supervision..." Sophia nodded and asked if there were any good clinics the doctor could recommend. The doctor said

"you should probably go back to Portugal and see about it there, it helps to know you're close to home, and he's going to need a lot of help, the poor guy"

At this he smiled and Sophia smiled too:

"thank you very much"

"welcome"

and the doctor tipped a hat that was not there and walked out of the cabin.

Father X coughed, causing Sophia to interrupt her story. This gave Father X a chance to speak.

"My dear, my poor dear, you've been through a terrible time"

"yes"

"but you're still strong"

"yes"

"you're still strong and you are going to survive, and so is your darling son, because that is what you must do, and for no other reason. Oh, Sophia, you know there is nothing I can say to undo all that has happened to you. And even if I could, it would not be my place to do so. We both understand how painful life can be, but we also both know that the good moments often outweigh the bad in their intensity. I cannot speak to you of God, because he is already with you, and with your son. You may wonder why our God hasn't acted to help you, but that is your question to ask, not mine. And I know you will never ask it, because you get it. Sophia, my dear, the truth is that what you are going through is unfair and tragic, and nobody would blame you for despairing; yet the young woman I remember from those many years ago seems to have remained inside you, and that is the highest compliment I can pay you and the greatest proof that something is *working* in the universe. You love your son as much as you possibly could. That is all you need to keep doing. Love him and let him feel your love, and let him take all the love he can. Never forget how ugly our lives would be if we wanted love but could never find it. Love him so much that he is forced to admit to himself that he is loved. Love him but love him subtly. Do not smother him. Do not insist. Simply show the love and let him take it as he wishes."

But there was nothing he could say to make her feel much better. Not that day, not with her sounding so sad. She was not miserable, or angry, or desperate any longer; it was only a quiet sadness and the need to talk that propelled her. She told him how she had checked her son into a hospital and sat by his side as he slept for one, two, three days, a full week, longer, until the doctors agreed that he had rested enough and they took the IV drip off and brought him some lunch. He didn't want to eat. He didn't feel awake enough for food. She held his hand and said

"how do you feel"

"I don't remember anything"

and it was as though he'd woken up after a car crash. The memories from the cruise would only come gradually. The doctor said Philippe would feel much better now and Sophia asked exactly what the next steps were, and the doctor explained that because it was still summer Philippe should take things slowly, maybe stay at home for another week or so, watch some TV, write in a journal if that helped, and get back on what the doctor called normal time, which is the number of hours during which one is most useful to society. The doctor said, too, that the new medication Philippe was on might cause a bit of weight gain, but it was nothing to worry about.

"but I do worry, I can't gain too much weight"

"you don't have to worry" the doctor said, and this settled the matter.

Father X didn't know what to say to Sophia, to my mother, the poor woman on the other end of the line whose emotions raged and flared and whose son sounded out of his mind. And I suppose my mother didn't know what to say to him now, either. She had needed the venting, the recklessness of confession, but what came next? What could they possibly say to each other now? So they exchanged empty words for a few minutes, and then Father X gave her more advice that she herself might have given, and soon there was simply nothing left to say.

FIVE

I used to tell my mother the ideas I had for novels I wanted to write. It was a traditional thing. The big novel, the one that would make my name, would be based, loosely, on the incident that had taken place on the cruise ship when I was fourteen. There was too much material there for me not to exploit it. Whatever she told Father X, she must not have known the full truth, which is as banal now as it was once destructive: I had fallen in love, as everyone does at some point of vulnerability, and on realizing that I had missed my big *chance*, the only opportunity to tell the girl what I *really felt*, that she would not be returning to my boarding school the following year, and that I would probably never see her again — in short, that life was exactly as difficult and stupid as I had guessed it to be — I cracked. This is what great novels are made of. Even I, who at fourteen had never read a great novel, knew that.

The habit I formed of talking to my mother about possible novels began not long before I had said goodbye to the young girl in question, whose name, Rima, filled me with a quiet sadness whenever it entered my thoughts. The name stood for every one of my failures: my lack of resolve, my cowardice, my timidity, my ugliness, everything that had helped me not to get the girl. Today there is an industry devoted to teaching young men how to seduce their favorite young women, but when it mattered most to me, the tools for such manipulation were not publicly avowed. I had nothing to help me except the example of my older peers, whom I did not like, and that of whatever father figure I had adopted at the time. The art of selecting one's words to seem a certain way was foreign to me. I did not have to choose my words because I rarely spoke to others, and when I did, it was with the kind of contempt that characterizes sociopaths. The more I disliked my classmates, the greater the gap between Rima and myself — how could it be otherwise? I was resolved not to lose the purity of my mind to any kind of contact with the people around me; this led to a lack of practice in the art of conversation; and when it counted — such as the ten or so times I ever really spoke to Rima — I was inept and maybe a little scary.

Speaking of scary: I remember in very great detail the first time that I spoke to my mother about my fiction. It was around the time of an important transformation. In short, not ten minutes after I had switched off the lights for the night, my skin started to peel, boils developed all over my knees, my hair crystallized, and my eyeballs froze. I suppose the only way to describe what happened is to allude to that thing we call the chrysalis. In a matter of minutes, my body became a cocoon. I was aware throughout of the weirdness of my condition. Yet I could do nothing about it. There was not an inch of my body that I could control, and because it was nighttime and my roommate was already asleep, prone as he was to overworking himself during the daytime, it was impossible to seek help. I was lying in my bed, but I was no longer a person on the outside. Within me the psychic spaces that I had once called my brain seemed deep and boundless.

I wondered, at first, if this were not punishment for my own failure, the failure to be myself, the failure to *become* myself. For so long I had felt that without Rima I would never be complete, and that I would never be with Rima unless I could complete myself around her — was this some strange revision of my destiny, an acceleration towards change prompted by an impatient god? Was this transformation something that I could have avoided if only I had dared to give in to my desires, to be exactly who I wanted to be? But that was impossible — I didn't know who I wanted to be, and I had no doubt that the person I would end up becoming would be monstrous, evil, a resentful failure. So was my cocooning a way for the order of things to correct me, to rework me into a thicker substance? I thought of my mother then, who was forever patient enough to repeat as many times as I needed that I was a good person, that I was an intelligent person, and that I would grow up to be a remarkable person. Only twenty minutes earlier, my mother had spent her energy convincing me that I was *not* ugly; that, in fact, I was better looking than most boys, and it always flattered her when acquaintances complimented her on having produced such a handsome young man. And what a polite young man. What an intelligent and likeable young man. Yet all this only emboldened my skepticism, and by the time she had run out of encouraging platitudes, I said if you only knew, if they knew what I really am, and my mother said what are you, really? And I told her: I told her that I was violent inside, that I was terribly alone, frightened by the idea of God, pesky and persistent God. I told her that I could not feel comfortable with myself, that I hated my acne, my belly, my hairy arms, my voice, my mind, my entire being. I loathed all of it unconditionally, and couldn't feel genuine unless I loathed it. And before I had said these things, I had believed them; but even as I spoke the words, I found myself unconvincing, as though by virtue of being said aloud the words became meaningless.

Was this altered state of being, the cocooning of my body, a kind of retribution, then, for all the things I had failed to do and the countless times I had hurt my mother? I wasn't so oblivious as to fail to realize that hearing me declare myself a monster was hard on her. It was cruel of me, and though it all seemed true and urgent, in the end there was no need to scare her like this. Through the appearance of my cocoon that night in my bed, perhaps God, who existed at the time, was exacting some cosmic punishment. But just as likely — and scarier, to me — was the possibility of this happening for no good reason. Maybe I was only suffering from being impotently alive in a universe that did not know itself. And if that was true, then there was no point in feeling sorry for myself. It was simply the way things worked.

Little by little the world inside my cocoon started to grow warmer and brighter. I lost contact with the world outside me, could no longer see the room or hear my roommate snoring. All I could see was white, the whitest and most perfect white, a white without bound or shape; there was nothing else, and because my vision stretched eternally into the bright abyss it was like looking at nothingness itself. The very ideas of form and order lost their importance. The heat, meanwhile, was growing stronger, and I felt the pressure of hot air against what I assumed was the inner wall of my cocoon. Perhaps, if any steam escaped through some crack, the whistling would wake my roommate. Sure enough, after a few minutes the heat was so intense that, had I owned a body of my own, I would have sweated myself to non-existence; the pressure around me got stronger than I could handle, and the whistling began just as I felt a decrease in consciousness. It was, I suspected, the very fabric of my being that was leaking out of the cocoon through a tiny aperture somewhere. With it went the heat, until I was too tired and cold to focus on finding a way out of there. I slept awhile.

When I woke I had transformed further. Whereas before I'd had no doubt that the cocoon was around me, and preventing my escape, now it seemed that I *was* the cocoon, encircling something more mysterious, a writhing and shrieking substance or creature. Perhaps the place of my consciousness had shifted from the body I had called mine to the cocoon, so that I was merely holding in what had once been me. I was like a baby holding in its stool, refusing to discard what could no longer be called necessary. Yet unlike a stool, the thing around which my mind had been wrapped was eager to break away, and quite possibly able. It kicked and tore at the cocoon walls, letting out howls of agony, and although I could feel nothing except the merest traces of pain — proof that I had not completely identified with the cocoon yet — I knew that the thing would not give up and possessed incredible strength. The more it scratched and punched and tried to rip the cocoon apart, the more suscep-tible I became to its attacks, until, about twenty minutes into this new stage, I felt every blow as though I truly had become the cocoon and the blows were aimed at my innards.

It was around this time, or perhaps a little later — the memory gets fuzzy now, because I was in so much pain — that whatever was inside me managed to break free. It ripped a hole in the chrysalis walls and lunged at the world outside, angrily sliding free from me and grunting as it landed on what were probably its feet. I could still see nothing outside of the space it had once occupied, so after it had left the room, there was a moment of utter silence that didn't end until I realized that what I had called my cocoon was now fizzling away, noiselessly, unhurriedly, like sparkling water. When the fizzling stopped and I had gained control of my body again — the fingers and the eyelids and the knees and everything else — I looked around the room. Nothing had changed, my roommate snored away, the darkness was total; but I was different. I stood and tiptoed to the bathroom across the hall, and looked in the mirror. The same face looked back. My hands, too, were the same, and as I urinated I wondered exactly what it was that felt odd. Like any dreamer woken by his own nightmare — though I'm still not sure I dreamed the whole thing — I barely thought about the dream itself, and focused instead on the secret thoughts that sleep had brought into the open. I spent the next two hours wide awake, taking intermittent trips to the bathroom just to look myself in the eyes and make sure I was still me.

In a large notepad I had bought for no good reason the term before, I put my ideas into words. The notion of radical, unprompted change appealed to me. More than that, it terrified me. What if the transformation had been real? How, then, might I find a way to get myself a girlfriend? And why, despite the other, more important implications of turning into a cocoon or some similarly repulsive thing, was my greatest concern to do with my romantic life? This was before I'd read any Kafka; I did not know exactly how immutable the human preoccupation with such mundane things really is. That I had had a nightmare was interesting enough — I rarely had them — but it was more unsettling to know that even during the nightmare I had thought of things like my love interest and my mother, instead of ways to get myself out of my situation or to communicate with my roommate for help. The most curious aspect of all was how quickly I had adapted to my new body and given up hope of turning back into a person. Deprived of my arms, legs and belly, I was free to roam in an unfamiliar psychic space, my thoughts circling around the things that, as a human, I had considered transcendentally important. I was, to put it simply, eternally human, even deprived of my humanity.

So I wrote my feelings down, and my thoughts, and my impressions, my memories of the dream. Seven pages later, I had an idea: Why not work this concept of mutability into the novel I had been trying to finish for the last six months? A novel completed at fourteen is never good, but it takes on such significance, and occupies so much emotional space in the life of its author, that it can't be dismissed out of hand.

My novel, a violent, complicated piece called *Bride*, revolved around a shooting in a boarding school eerily similar to mine. The two protagonists, Jason Packard and Harvey Bride, were opposed in most ways: Packard was kind, Bride was not; Packard was constantly in danger of being expelled, Bride kept to himself; while Packard was lonely despite his active social life, Bride was alone because he could not relate to others at all. They were not friends. Packard, the troublemaker, was the obvious hero of the story: he maintained decent relations with people, stood up for himself, and actively fought teenage injustices. Bride was rather more problematic. He had been bullied for so long, beaten by his peers and ignored by his teachers, that his only goal was to find the means to put a bullet in everybody's head. With his black friend Hoofie, not too loosely based on my own black friend at the time, Bride stayed under the radar for as long as possible until the fateful date when, with a gun he'd purchased from a local thug, he would at last get his revenge on the world.

The novel was poorly written for the most part. Rereading it now, however, I get the feeling that the sentiments driving its composition — the anger and the solitude, the will to get back at a universe that seemed not to make any sense at all — were all genuine. Who represented me more accurately, Packard or Bride? Would I have been capable of murdering my classmates simply because I could not relate to them? I have never allowed anyone to read *Bride* in full. The shame of admitting to myself how little I knew about myself and the world, combined with the worry of being locked in a cell somewhere in case I ever feel like enacting the story's bloody climax, has stopped me from even telling people about the novel. I did, however, discuss the development of the manuscript with my mother — at least some parts of the manuscript.

I never told her, for instance, that I was writing in two voices: that of Packard, the lone fighter for good, and that of Bride, the mastermind behind a terrible rampage in a boarding school gymnasium. As far as she knew, there was only Packard, who discovered Bride's plans and tried his hardest to stop the shooting from taking place, and succeeded. The truth was less attractive, and I wasn't naive enough to think she would be pleased to learn that the shooting did take place in the context of the novel. Nor did I make the mistake of telling her that the students in the novel were based on my own classmates, and that most of the novel was narrated by Bride, not Packard. This was a would-be murderer's manifesto.

It was the cocoon dream that prompted me to talk to my mother about the novel in any kind of depth. Something inside me had been dislodged. I wanted to break out of my cycles of self-pity and anger at the world. The first step was to talk about something new with my mother, who was an admirable encourager but on whom I had come to rely too much for my sense of identity. If every time we spoke on the phone, she sank back into the role of enlightened parent, who could tell me sweet things forever without tiring, then I would not be able to find my own way of being myself, whatever that meant. So I decided to treat her as the human being that, over time, I had discovered she was. It's common, or at least I hope it's common, to feel deep shame when you realize your parents are as deluded and naive as everyone else; but my strategy, in dealing with this realization, had so far been to act as if the illusion had never shattered. I told her my problems — except the truly embarrassing ones, like the Rima situation — and she listened and she said kiddo, you worry too much, have you been getting enough exercise, and so on. We had never gone beyond the superficiality of infant love, which, though deep in its way, is love for no reason at all, and therefore perhaps the closest thing to purity — what I mean is that it's boring. Growing up means loving for selfish reasons; we know this. After the cocoon dream, I resolved to let her see the darker side of the thing she knew as her darling kiddo.

The idea of having been turned into a cocoon, however briefly, had unsettled me, and I felt a renewed lust for Rima, an emboldened desire to make the adults around me proud, and, less promisingly, a greater contempt for my peers than ever before. I was fourteen and, like every fourteen-year-old, I believed myself wiser than my years. I would prove everyone wrong, though I wasn't sure exactly how they were wrong, or if they cared, or whether they would even notice. It was such feelings of isolation that had led me to begin my novel. Now that I had about one hundred pages stored on my computer, it was time to get my mother involved. She would know how to improve the story. As long as I kept the most important details hidden from her, and only asked vague questions about plot structure, perhaps, then she'd be happy to help and I wouldn't feel so horribly alone.

When the moment came to explain to my mother what I was trying to do with the manuscript, my cowardice won out. Without telling her the dirty details — the focus on revenge, Bride's insane rants at the reader about the injustice of life, and the planned climax involving countless deaths — there was no point in talking about it at all. So that morning after the cocoon dream, I told her I was writing something else, something far less risqué than a school-shooting novel. I described the imaginary novel in very great depth, making everything up as I went along; and my mother seemed so delighted to hear it that she seemed not to suspect anything more sinister was taking place in her baby's head. I came up with so many ideas for this hypothetical novel, so many ridiculous, childish and suitably innocent ideas, that by the end of the conversation I felt convinced that it was my calling to write the damned thing. I put the *Bride* manuscript aside and worked on the new story until the end of the school year. It was only when I saw Rima for the last time, beautiful and chubby and blonde and sunlit, that the rage truly welled up in me again. By the time I'd said farewell to her, I was crazed with fury: I had let myself be sidetracked by this stupid new novel, a novel that had actually been fun to write. Fun! I had wasted my last three weeks of grade eight by writing something that had begun as a bluff anyway, and failed to do the only thing that I thought mattered: Tell Rima. Tell her everything. Somehow that would make things better.

Not long after the summer began, my mother broke her ankle in Portugal. She'd tripped over a large rock at my grandfather's farm, and the swelling was considerable. The doctors said there was nothing better in such cases than letting the swelling subside, relaxing, *taking it easy*, as the Portuguese doctors were so fond of saying in English. Since my sister was meant to go to summer camp in the Alps, my mother decided to take me there too, so we could all enjoy the alpine air and so her foot could heal. I followed them to the mountains in silence, saying very little either on the flight or at dinner the night we arrived. Rima obsessed me. Idiot, you let her go. You felt you almost had her at times, but you lost your nerve. You are a coward. You'll never see her again. This is the end of that, but you can't let it die.

It was my only bout of writer's madness. For the three weeks we spent in Switzerland, I saw no friends, ate almost no food, and got little sleep. After installing my laptop in the chalet's attic, I told my mother not to disturb me unless she needed me to push her wheelchair around. I sought no company from anyone, I said, and she smiled in confusion. Then I left her and took a few sips from one of the bottles of vodka in the living room, looking over my shoulder all the while, and rushed upstairs to complete the story of Jason Packard and Harvey Bride.

Three weeks of doing nothing but destroying my keyboard and developing the plot. Suddenly and mysteriously, I introduced a love interest in the Packard narrative. When that subplot started to consume too much space, and when I noticed that every scene involving Packard and his girlfriend was a way for me to pretend I had succeeded with Rima, I deleted ten thousand words of my manuscript, and plowed onwards. I typed and spat into a mug and drank from the vodka in the living room. When it got too sunny outside I closed the blinds. Whenever my mother asked me to help her get from one floor of the house to another, I did so grudgingly, as though she had played a part in my mental collapse — and that was was it felt like: an endless collapse, as though the foundations of my mind were so enormous that when they began to fall, they never quite managed to reach the bottom of the abyss. I would sit there and type, get up and help my mother go to the bathroom, then sit down and type again, churning out pages faster than I ever would again. It felt a careless, joyful exercise in self-negation, an excuse to forget my immediate problems and everything that made me who I am, and instead to create the illusion of order in the lives of my characters. Every character was part of me. I found myself splitting my imagination into little infinities, each a character and a scene and a combination of words. It was the first time in my life I could pretend without consequences. There was nobody to call me on my bluff, because no one was around me. Whenever my mother asked what I was doing, up there in the attic on my own, in the dark, in the heat, I told her I was writing, and refused to answer any more questions. With her broken ankle she couldn't come up to check on me. It was the perfect arrangement.

My return key fell off on the day that I finished *Bride*. The story was exactly as dark and violent as I wanted it. I had described, in no doubt too much detail, the events leading to Harvey Bride's death at the hands of good-guy Jason Packard: the meticulous planning, the ranting in front of a terrified audience of students taken by surprise, the firing of the first shots, the blood seeping out of a young man's head, the chaos, the unexpected fire, the showdown between Packard and Bride, and Packard's victory in the midst of violent flames. Everything was excessive, hysterical and furious; my state of mind at the point of the novel's completion was one to look out for in troubled teenagers; though I'd never consciously been tempted to shoot my friends down in an act of sadism or revenge, all evidence to be found in my novel — and that was plenty of evidence — pointed to the disturbing possibility that I was, in a word, unwell.

Nor did I fail to see it. After a couple of days of rest, moments of sunlit walks and being around my lonesome mother, I grasped just how sick I must be to have written — and to have enjoyed writing — such a damnable and grotesque novel. The characters were all based on my own friends and teacher; Bride and Packard shared incredible similarities with their author; and the number of students in my boarding school — 180 — was exactly the number of students in the school Packard and Bride attended. It was fiction based on facts, and such fiction brought out the most terrible fact of all: I was a monster.

My mother did not treat me like a monster. She had no interest in writing her own fiction, but she often asked about mine. Her questions were always pertinent.

"what's the point of this or that character" she'd ask

and I'd say "he doesn't really have a purpose"

"then why is he in the story"

"because that's life"

"how so"

"does everyone you meet become an important character in your life-story"

"no"

"then you see what I mean"

"but it's confusing for the reader"

"yes but the reader will adapt"

"so what are you trying to achieve here"

"nothing in particular, I guess"

"well, I think you should learn to leave certain things out"

"like what"

"like useless characters"

"I know, you're right"

and she'd say: "how about you rewrite it"

"I know that I should, but it's a lot of work"

"I've heard all the great authors have rewritten their books until they became different books"

"and I said: yes but I want to have something to say, mom"

"you have so many things to say, you're a smart child, kiddo"

"I have only anger, that's the only thing that makes me write"

"you've written some very funny stories"

"but those came from my anger"

"so write your anger out"

"it never helps"

"well, whatever you do, keep writing, because you are good

at it"

"does it make you proud"

"yes, of course it does, but it also makes me less worried about you, since you can get it all out when you write"

Life would have been easier if I'd only spoken to my mother about this, instead of imagining conversations. As it happened, I waited until I was eighteen and more or less stable and conventionally *socialized* to tell her why I had been in so much pain a few years before. The scene, in fact, was comical and even absurd, and it was only when I'd said the words — I was in love with a girl when all that drama happened — that I was able to accept how grotesquely human I'd turned out to be. A few months before I graduated from high school, my mother flew to Switzerland to discuss various things with some of my teachers, and to see her beloved son. The Saturday afternoon when she got there, I took her to a pizzeria. She ate a salad and listened as I said: I have to confess something to you.

Confess? What was there to confess? All I wanted was to say aloud what I'd known for years and thought she should know: that for every *I don't know* or *I can't explain it* she should have listened for yet another *I am in love.* So I told her: when we were on the cruise ship and I was going all crazy, I was in love with a girl in my school. Her name was Rima and she was on my mind absolutely all of the time. It was an obsession. I felt terrified and I knew that I wasn't acting the way normal people act. I took everything too seriously. I am completely certain that we should link the day I said goodbye to Rima and received only a friendly peck on the cheek to the day I started to smell those burning onions and getting paranoid. It was only ten days from the peck on the cheek to the breakdown on the ship. Does that sound weird to you too? That I was able to contain my demons for that long because there was always a stupid hope in my heart that I'd be able to *confess* to her that I loved her — and that the moment I understood I had failed, and that Rima would not be returning to that school the following year, I broke down — is this not obvious?

My mother listened sadly, smiling a little, looking at the plate before her instead of at me. What to say to this kiddo, this deluded, romantic eighteen-year-old kid who'd brought her so much joy and pain? She finally looked up and said: you've always been ashamed of falling in love. You asked me once, when you were maybe four years old, what love was, and every time you said the word, you giggled as though you were doing something naughty. And I never understood why, when you went off to boarding school, you refused to speak about anything to do with love. Did you notice that? Are you aware this is the first time you've ever spoken to me about a crush? You've had girlfriends, and you're happy to let me meet those, but you never say that you *like* them to me. It's always been out of bounds.

(But this wasn't a crush, mother. This was a full-blown obsession. You saw what I was like on the ship. I couldn't have been less stable. And the whole time that I was suffering, I was suffering because of her.)

You weren't suffering because of her, kiddo. You can't have been suffering because of her when you knew so little about who she was. You didn't even know yourself. I think you're making sense of all of what happened back then by finding an overarching explanation. And that's good, as long as you understand that you were dealing with much more than just the ghost of a pretty girl. When I was thirteen, I tried to cut my wrists — did you know that? I was vulnerable, and my parents were getting divorced, and things were tense in the house, so tense that I couldn't feel safe. And I tried to cut a wrist, but I didn't cut deeply enough. (Which wrist?) This one. You can't even see the scar anymore unless you really look hard. But the reason I'm telling you this is so you know that being miserable when you're thirteen, fourteen, is perfectly legitimate. People don't tend to think that teenagers have *good* reasons to commit suicide — they assume teenagers do it for the attention, or because they're just immature. But when you're that young — fourteen, thirteen, twelve — it doesn't matter why you're doing it. Something's happening inside you that is unpleasant and horrifying.

(I suppose. I suppose you're right. But what if I'm just going to be like this forever? What if, every time I find someone fascinating and beautiful the way I found Rima to be fascinating, beautiful and so much more, what if every time that happens I end up obsessing and destroying myself? Should I be concerned about my well-being? Shouldn't you be, too?)

Not if you're aware of all of it. Kiddo, I know it's not easy for you to understand this on anything other than an intellectual level, because it feels so deeply entrenched in you, but I'll still say it: if you are capable of seeing your thoughts an unreasonable, you are not losing your mind. That's the first thing a sane person does: they wonder if they're going crazy. You know that a crazy person doesn't think they're crazy. And you are still young and you are impatient to grow up and be, well, *normal*, but I know you know there's no such thing as being perfectly balanced. There are degrees of imbalance, and you're sorting yourself out. One of the things I've found as I've grown older is that the older you get, the less sensitive you become. And I think that's a good thing. When I was young and too sensitive to be helpful to anyone, I took everything seriously. Everything. My parents' divorce seemed like the worst thing in the world. It wasn't. But because I couldn't *help* but feel that it was, I found myself incapable of functioning like the adults I admired. And I wanted to be like them. I wanted to sound as though I knew what I was doing, saying, thinking, feeling. Now I'm the age they were back then, and I know that they knew no better than I did. The difference was that they didn't mind that so much. They just didn't mind it.

SIX

I can let go of my mother's life — it is gone, I have no choice. The problem is in understanding, not the void she left, but the nature of the void, the shape of the crater now that the debris is covered in flora. Why do some things about her death bother me more now than they did when the wound was fresh? Why am I no longer haunted by certain images, terrifying as I once found them, while others have resurfaced, perhaps out of pure imagination? And when, if ever, will I so entirely forget what life with her was like that she will seem no more real than a character out of a novel?

Because none of us was prepared for her sudden departure, least of all she herself, her death was like an act of terrorism on a previously calm day. She died, everything erupted into flame, we put the fire out, and then the death became real, and we felt threatened, alone, no longer able to see the world the same way. Nobody had anticipated it — should we have examined every artery in her head to make sure one would not burst? — so when it happened, the blow was only felt after the danger was over, and the agony lingered. And yet, though there has been no end to the horror of the world being motherless, everything is creeping back to normal. I find new ways of mourning and cannot let go of the suffering, it only feels correct to writhe, but I am again attending to daily chores, making new promises to new people, and the mourning has become a new way of being, purposeless, leading to no loosening of the knot. I am mourning because it feels good to mourn, because it prolongs the pain.

And this baffles me — I suppose this is no way to grieve, but it feels like the only honest way to do it. If she were on a trip somewhere and I could expect her back soon, I would give her no thought at all; still she won't be back and I have years of missing her ahead of me. Hard to tell now if this pleasure I feel from mourning her will turn into something new. She is on a very long trip. She will not return except in memories and dreams. It is as if our lives had been reversed: now she goes off to boarding school for a year at a time, and I sit here in this kitchen and wait for her to return. Perhaps she will find a boyfriend. Perhaps she will do well in her exams. As long as she is happy. As long as she's coming back, and doesn't forget that I raised her, that I love her...

This kitchen will be the first place to spend a bit of time. This kitchen in our little house in a little village in tiny Portugal. Marble tiles on the floor, dark and cold. My mother used to walk around here in her slippers. I never saw her barefoot. Her feet got cold. She was always cold. And that explains the little portable heater that we kept in the kitchen sometimes, in case it got so chilly that my mother couldn't take it. This kitchen is the first place to sit and think everything through. How many conversations I had with her in here. I was seventeen, eighteen, a little older or younger, back from boarding school, eating cereal at this table, with a napkin under my bowl so it wouldn't stain the table-cloth...

"but it doesn't matter if the tablecloth gets stained, mom"

"it does, it's just been washed"

"but it's milk"

"hush, kiddo"

... cereal that she bought every few days so we never ran out. Whatever cereal you like, she said. I'm glad to have you home.

And I was glad to be home. Because when I came home from Switzerland, when it was time to enjoy my holidays and play video games and read books, record music, cuddle with the cats, see my beautiful mother — when I came home it was always good simply to see how little my mother had changed. Still poised, still so wise. Dating that Ukrainian man, an electrician; spending hours on the phone sorting out all varieties of family troubles; telling me that she loved me, kiddo. And I love you.

And I was a mama's boy for a few weeks, before returning to that excessive environment in the Alps, with the snow that I hated and the adolescent boredom. I was glad to be home and I savored it.

When the holidays were over I had to go back to Switzerland, and leave her to her routines and her life without me. While I was away, experiencing the awkwardness of crushes that seemed to drag on eternally, or looking for things to distract me from the grind of feeling superior to everyone and impossibly weak, she was just *there*. Doing things one at a time. Worrying about me, in this kitchen, sipping her decaffeinated coffee. Of course it was decaf — she had enough trouble sleeping:

"then why drink coffee at all" I'd say

"because even decaf has a bit of caffeine"

"that's ridiculous"

"yeah, yeah"

Sipping decaf and reading the newspaper. She only ever read the International Herald Tribune. And it was always in the kitchen, during the few moments of peace the world granted her.

The kitchen was the place I told her about most developments in my life away from home. In fact kitchens were often our favorite place simply to learn about each other. This is true of the kitchen in every house we occupied. In London, when I was eight, I ate twenty-six — maybe twenty-seven — tangerines in the space of a half-hour. The goal was to turn orange, as my mother had warned me that I would if I carried on eating so many of those things. I reached a critical point, and vomited; my mother, who had been on the phone, came in and sighed. She cleaned up the mess, put me in the bath, and never bought so many tangerines again.

I see all the kitchens in all the places we lived even now, see some of them better than I can remember my mother's eyes. Other memories surge up from time to time, but those kitchens covered in messes I'd made while trying to cook, those kitchens with three jars of peanut butter lying empty on their sides by the sink, those are the memories that don't leave me feeling down. My mother was forever sighing, forever cleaning plate after plate, picking up the phone and hanging up and wiping the plates again. The maid came every day to help but still my sister and I made messes everywhere. So they'd scrub, crouch onto the floor to clean up some spilt juice, stand on a chair to change the bulbs, my mother listening to the maid's blabber, the maid ignoring everything my mother said. And when all was clean for at least a couple of hours, it was back to reading the paper in the kitchen. This was the ritual. Take care of business, have a decaf, take care of more business — retire to the kitchen.

I have never learned to cook — my skills end with a rudimentary steak. But when my mother tried to teach me how to mix cream with Dijon mustard to make a sauce everyone particularly enjoyed, or when she showed me the correct way to pour Madeira wine into a pan full of frying meat, I felt a bond with her stronger than any other, and it was because we were in the kitchen, doing something I cared nothing about in theory, but enjoying it still because we were together and loved each other. There was no good reason to teach me these things, useful as they might later have proven to be. She would show me how to open a bottle with a corkscrew, and I would try it out, then forget about it at once. She'd tell me the secret to knowing when to turn a steak over — she, the near-vegetarian who only ate meat because of her anemia — so that it was just bloody enough for me to enjoy, and I would pretend to learn. Then it was out of my head. Who cares about steak? I go to boarding school. My meals are all cooked for me. And many of them are even quite good. I do this for your pleasure, mother — and for mine, for I love you.

It was in the kitchen that I told my mother intimate things, and it was in the kitchen that I hid the most important things as well. My mother sat at the table with a newspaper in her hands. Asking about my time at school, listening sadly as I told her all the banalities of a schoolboy's life except, no doubt, the ones she would have most liked to help me with: my obsessive admiration for a beautiful student, my ideas of suicide the origins of which I could barely identify. What little savvy I had when it came to dealing with her — the intuition that revealing my suicidal thoughts would only cause her intolerable pain, for instance — meant that I kept from her everything she would have paid any price to know. And for her protection; I did not wish to make her suffer, so I shut her out from all these things which, thinking back, I realize I should have burdened her with.

Mother, I am sad. It's not a crush, it's not a schoolboy fantasy that's killing me; I am miserably, helplessly infatuated and I want help. I want to talk to you about it, but to admit this, to confess that I am capable of sexual feelings at the age of fourteen — which would come as no shock to you, but I don't know this — to confess this would be so humiliating, would make me feel like such an embarrassing failure, that I choose instead to bury it all inside me. And now you are shut out. You can't help because I have given you no clues. Instead, we cook together and I tell you about books I'm reading, stories I'm writing, grades I am attaining, things you can be proud of me for. I tell you who my friends are, what sports the gym teachers are forcing me to try, which mountains surround my school and how bright the snow on them is in winter. I tell you this — I say everything you want to hear from a happy son. I will give you every detail, as long as it means nothing to me. How wonderful the library is, with a curious selection of books that no student ever reads, from *Ulysses* to the Bible, Dante and Dostoevsky. People don't read at my school. They drink vodka on the sly — but I don't tell you that, because I'm not one of those kids. I do read. I read all the time, I read every book you tell me to read. You told me to read *Lord Arthur Saville's Crime* so I took it out from the library and I read it. Now I will tell you my thoughts on it. I already knew the twist because you'd told me, but what a great story.

And thank you for recommending Vercors's little masterpiece, *Le silence de la mer*, which I read in one go on a camping trip with classmates I was trying not to mingle with. It is a great book. I wish I'd written it. I wish, sort of, that you could read my darker stories — the stories full of psychical bloodshed, the torment, hatred and loneliness. But you won't. You'll suspect I am unhappy, see it in how I react to the world, but you won't know for sure until I implode. A total meltdown. You'll see the thing you raised break apart and despise you.

I'm sorry I haven't written you any emails lately. I'm sorry I don't call you more often. The day I turned fourteen I decided not to call home more than once a week. It feels unmanly to do it. I want to be a man. Do you want to know what I'm up to when I'm not in the kitchen with you, cooking or making smoothies? When you are home and I'm in Switzerland so far from you and from my sister — when I'm not calling because I don't want to alarm you, even though I do want to alarm you, because I want you to know all isn't well, all is shit, but you can't know, even though you should know, even if I don't tell you, because you are my mom. What I'm up to when you're in Portugal and I'm up in the mountains is nothing special. I'm writing my way out of my boredom. I am a clumsy writer, but I write. I don't write to *you*, or to anyone in particular, but I write. I write not to create wonderful literature, but to avoid murdering, to stop myself from disappearing completely. I wish you'd read my *real* writing, the serious stuff, the stuff you'd send me to a psychiatrist for, but I don't let you. I discuss stories with you all the time. You make for excellent conversation about this because you don't write, but you read. You care. I really should let you read the darkness. Maybe you'd even get it. Probably. You'd understand that I think obsessively about a girl, you'd get why I avoid other students. In fact — how about I just tell you? You can read this now, read the truth of what your kid's going through. You deserve to know because you want to help. You always want to help. It's simply humiliating. That's all. I can deal with humiliation. I just can't deal with myself.

Mom. The signal's breaking up. Can you hear me? I can hear *you*. I'm fine. What's wrong?

And you tell me not to worry if I hear bad news about America. What bad news? And you tell me there's been an attack, planes. It is my first week in this school, I have no friends yet, I am trying to make friends and I have no idea why I should be concerned with any of this — we are not in America — why is this such a big deal? You tell me not to worry and I'm not worried. But your voice unsettles me. We have cousins in New York. I haven't met them. Mom — I want to tell you about a girl I see from time to time around campus, a lovely girl. That's what's on my mind. Who cares about America? Why are you so concerned? I am not thinking of anything else, just the sight of this girl, the phantom of possible love. But I won't tell you because that would be admitting I am capable of affection for others, which, for reasons I can't admit to myself, sounds unlike the me you know. So I listen to your concerns about America. How the school will probably explain what's happening once anyone really knows. Fine. Mom, I don't like hearing you sound like this — worried, scared, almost stupid. Be yourself again.

And as America loses its fragile sanity, so does the rest of the world. I stop paying attention. The next time I'm back in the kitchen with my mother, it is a winter's day; school has ended for the holidays.

"how are your friends"

"they're fine"

"but what are they like"

"I haven't made many"

"but you have a few good ones at least"

"yes"

"and what are they like"

"they're okay, they don't annoy me"

"good"

(I don't want to tell you about my friends. I want to talk to you about things I find interesting, baffling: I am not good at mathematics but that's what you teach at university. Tell me about it, Mom. What is an imaginary number? Aren't all numbers imaginary, if I can't actually see them in the real world? Isn't infinity just a bigger number than we can count to in all our lifetimes? What is category theory? What is topology? Why are you sighing?)

"and how are your classes"

"you ask me this every time we talk on the phone"

"I know, but phone conversations are so short"

"I told you, classes are fine"

"okay, if you don't want to talk about school, we don't have to"

"just don't ask so many questions"

(Don't ask me about my social life, at least. I have none. I am happy this way. I'm not happy this way but I'm *myself* this way.)

I can't bear to be in this kitchen much longer. There's nothing here anymore. No food in the cupboards, just empty bottles, old salt, a crack in one of the chairs from the time the dogs got too excited and jumped up onto my mother while she was eating her soup. I can walk around, put my hand to the wall, feel the surfaces of things; but none of this makes the kitchen as I remember it. This is hardly a kitchen at all. It is structured like one, but nobody cooks in it these days. Nobody sits and reads the newspaper. No dogs sleeping under the table. No smell of coffee, decaffeinated and only lukewarm, as she liked it. I am pacing but achieving nothing. Open the drawers — knives, forks, spoons that haven't been used in a year and won't be used for a long time yet. All of them very clean, very shiny. There is a box full of old dark chocolate that nobody is going to eat, because only she enjoyed dark chocolate around here. The box is sitting on the counter next to a blender she only used when I was around, for my smoothies. Because they are healthy. You can drink them all you like. You can drink smoothie after smoothie and I'll keep making them for you, because I love you, kiddo.

Christ, I wish the world knew what it was missing.

SEVEN

I am prey to that stupid habit, common in those who get off on telling themselves lies, of trying endlessly and tirelessly to arrive at conclusions about the past. Because the past seems so inconclusive, so full of little uncertainties that grow bigger every time one thinks about them, it becomes almost a game to see if a knot can be tied around the past to choke it, kill it and examine the contents of everything that has been without worrying about it biting back. Such is my masturbatory joy in sandpapering the edges of the pieces of the puzzle so that they'll fit wherever I stick them — such is this joy that I would be lying if I claimed to want the truth. I don't care how things actually happened. I want to rearrange it all, to make it into a streamlined, coherent narrative. And very often this tactic works. I work out when and where things went wrong with a friend; or I plot the ups and downs of a particular love affair, and grant an added importance to a scene that ought to have been more climactic when it took place. I am a scavenger of my own past, because I feel no remorse at altering the events that I believe made me blossom — or wilt — into this man.

The unfortunate consequence of this craftsmanship is the blurring effect it's had on my memory of events; when I really do need to remember how exactly something happened, I can't say with any conviction what is true and what is embellishment. This is particularly troubling as I write this because I can't remember how it all happened, that night when I stopped functioning like a budding fifteen-year-old adult and felt the universe collapse. I was in my fancy Alpine boarding school. I had few friends, and I looked for male role models in certain of the staff members there. And I know that my breakdown had a great deal to do with the loss of the most important of those role models. The trouble lies in recalling what was going through my mind when I found myself stripped of what I can only call his qualified friendship, his leadership, his erratic help.

I had sought companionship from a man whose presence was terrifying and inspiring, the man they called Samson at my school. A complicated man. Not a fan of political correctness. Samson insulted students left and right, to desensitize them, to instill some courage in those little fuckers. And little fuckers is exactly what we were. This man had more flaws than anyone I'd ever met. When he wasn't punishing a student for some offense he cared little about, he was running the school in a hundred other ways; but he did it clumsily, sadly, taking sips from a mug of coffee spiked with whisky, sighing, rolling his eyes, hating being there. A man with permanent stubble and a green tie around his neck whenever he taught his classes once a week; otherwise he wore baggy t-shirts covering up an enormous belly that failed to make the rest of him look fat.

He was crass —

"you fucking better get yourselves to class on time this week"

and he was angry —

"get off the phone, it's lights out... I don't care if it's your grandfather on the phone, I don't care if it's the fucking pope on the phone, it's lights out now"

and he was strangely seductive if he wanted to be. When parents were around he looked his best, stayed off the whisky — why do alcoholics only drink whisky? — and acted about as professional as he could. We weren't fooled, we, the boys he looked after, the terrified teenage kids who knew that as soon as it was bedtime, we'd have nothing to look forward to except a night of restlessness and Samson's preferred method for waking us up: a smack on the back and then a twist of the nipples, until we yelped out. It was his game, his way of ensuring that you kids are bright awake already, now get in the showers, put your uniform on, go to breakfast, and get to class on time this week, you understand? And he would storm around from room to room with that mug in his hand and a smile on that mug, saying:

"get up, get up, come on"

giving each kid a nickname; mine was Sulky:

"come on, Sulky, get dressed, and open the windows, it stinks in this room"

And he'd open the windows himself and smirk.

Samson picked his favorites and invited them to his apartment after lights out to smoke cigars and talk about girls. I was never a favorite — I was too intense, too unreliable in his eyes; how could he be sure I wasn't planning on being the one to break the silence, to tell the school was Samson was up to at night, smoking cigars and telling his favorites about the world? Of all the little weirdoes he had to take care of, I was the one likeliest to crack. The one whose conscience would get the better of him, the one whose jealousy could lead him to rat on the others. So he treated me with occasional kindness but I was not part of his clan.

He told us to carry blades and follow the law, and we didn't know what he meant but it sounded epic.

"do you think you're trying hard enough to be happy" he asked me one day in the hallway.

I said:

"what do you mean"

"do you even try to be happy"

"why are you asking me this"

"because I'm sick of seeing you moping around, Phil"

"I'm not moping around"

"here's a secret: if you want to be happy, you have to live for something outside of yourself, that's just how happiness works, it creeps in when you're busy doing something else"

"thank you for the advice"

"you're not listening to me"

"I feel picked on"

"Christ, I'm not picking on you, grow up"

"I..."

"you what"

"I want to grow up but I don't want to be picked on, not by you"

"Jesus Christ, nobody's picking on you, look, I'm trying to explain to you that you need to step out of your head and fight for something, that's all, pick a sport, find a hobby, something"

"I have a hobby"

"what is it"

"I write"

"what do you write"

"stuff, fiction"

"well, that's a start, but it's still so narcissistic, why can't you do something a little more social, start a pingpong club"

"I hate pingpong"

"only because you think you're too clever for sports"

"no, I just don't like pingpong"

and he sighed and walked off, perhaps to pour more whisky into his coffee.

Sometimes he woke us up with his water gun, spraying us in the face and pulling us out of bed, laughing and hooting. Then he'd spend the day looking tired and hung-over. Whenever the school board reprimanded him for his unorthodoxy, he nodded seriously and walked away determined to discipline us in less controversial ways. It was only so long, though, before he was back to hurling insults and spraying us with water and twisting our nipples and calling us by our assigned nicknames.

A whispered rumor went round: he had children somewhere back home. I never dared to ask him about this. But he had no trouble speaking about my mother to me. For reasons that remain cloudy and weird even now, Samson never much cared for my mother. From the first time she and I visited that boarding school, he took an intense, almost irrational dislike to her. But, manipulator and qualified professional that he was, he was consistently polite, friendly and considerate when she was around. It was when he and I were alone in his office that he deigned to alert me to her shortcomings as a parent:

"she overprotects you, you know"

"I know she does"

"she's always calling us to make sure you're okay, she thinks you're depressed"

and I, shocked to learn this, would say:

"how often does she call"

"sometimes as often as once a week, just to make sure you're okay, and I have better things to do than reassure your mother that you're not going to kill yourself; you're not going to kill yourself, are you"

"of course not"

"then for fuck's sake, tell your mother nice things when you speak to her on the phone, because I am sick of telling mommy that baby is not depressed"

"but how do you know"

"how do I know *what*"

"that I'm not depressed"

"oh for the love of our almighty motherfucking father, you really are a little narcissist, aren't you"

"what do you mean"

"nobody gets depressed at fourteen"

"is that so"

"yes, that is so, Phil, nobody is smart enough to understand anything important enough to be depressing at the age of fourteen"

"I am *fifteen*"

"see, this is why I still think you're immature"

"what"

"you think a year makes a difference, really, do you really think it matters whether you're fourteen or fifteen"

"I don't feel well, though"

"uh huh, and I've told you if you do some fucking *sports* you'll feel better"

"it's always sports, sir, I wish you wouldn't insist on sports, I hate sports"

"you hate sports because you're afraid of competition"

"not true"

"it's true, and you know it, you are afraid of getting down and dirty with other students because you look down upon them"

"no, I just don't like sweating"

"get out of here"

His advice was to accept my condition and move on. Do sports. Get a girlfriend. One day he didn't seem to care whether I got better; the next he wanted to make me improve as though his sanity depended on it. Look, he said, you have to figure this out. Maybe you'll always be like this. Maybe you are just an oversensitive kid now, or maybe you'll always be oversensitive. I don't know. But you really gotta work on things. You gotta learn yourself through and through, find out what makes you anxious, what really pisses you off. Then you know what to expect when those things happen. Living well takes practice, you know. It's not all a ride that someone is going to take you on; you gotta take yourself on a path, even if it's a fucked up path. You're such an idealist, it's gonna kill you, you know. You get depressed whenever you hear a girl burp. That's ridiculous, Sulky. You need to accept that people are disgusting things and that the good in people doesn't lie in their politeness. Otherwise, well, you are going to be miserable for a long time.

I trusted Samson. He could be tender with us when he thought we needed it, and he did it better than anyone around. Sometimes he rolled his eyes and told me to go do some sports; but when he saw circles under my eyes and knew I'd had a sleepless night, he would take me aside: You sleeping okay? What's going on? And I told him the anxiety was keeping me up at night.

"I can't sleep"

"what's going through your mind when you can't sleep"

"I don't know"

"well, do you need anything"

"I'm starving"

"then go eat"

and he'd pat me on the back and give me a friendly smile.

The king of duality, this man could be saintly one minute and tyrannical the next, shifting without warning, sliding in and out of foulness with every sip of his whisky. How did this man, this torturer, alcoholic, charmer, ugly-handsome, educated, this vulgar but good-hearted man manage to destroy himself so thoroughly? What led him to drink just that little bit too much, that final drop, the one that brought about the end of our contact with him? That night — that coffee spiked with whisky — Samson alone in his apartment at three in the morning with Little Richard playing on the stereo: What the fuck. Drinking himself to sleep again, horny, confused, Little Richard's voice telling the world about music. He is drunk, he needs to do something he has not allowed himself to do until now. Those little wrists. Samson, taking that sip, decides it's time, it's time to just get it the fuck over with, it's three in the morning and who's going to give a damn? The little bastard is asking for it anyway. Jealous little bastard, little faggot, is going to feel these hands and know what's up. Not his cock, not Samson's cock. Someone else's cock, some little faggot, it's three in the morning and we are too God damned drunk to care about tiny favors, aren't we. Walks up the stairs in the darkness and feels around for the little faggot's door. Opens it and creeps inside, he can hear the kid snoring. Kids shouldn't snore or they're not kids. This little fucking annoying shitty little prick, sleeping in his faggot bed. Samson sits on the side of the bed, slides his hand under the covers and leads it to the warmth of the little faggot's crotch. A firm grasp of those balls.

I discovered later, after we'd all received a letter during a school break explaining that Samson had chosen to resign from his position because of problems of a personal nature, that one of my friends, one of Samson's favorites, had woken to find this terrifying drunken man masturbating while fondling my friend's testicles. This information was never disclosed officially by the school — as far as anyone else knew, Samson had simply decided to check into rehab because of his famous drinking problem. (The headmaster offered my friend's family a hefty amount of money to keep what had happened a secret. The family refused; but they agreed to stay quiet.) To learn all of this, to absorb it and think deep down that none of it was really surprising, that in fact nothing about it seemed extraordinary at all, it was just how things would have ended up being anyway — to feel such indifference, such a mixture of relief and sadness and sheer indifference...

But indifference quickly turned to bitterness, then helplessness, and finally to something urgent and ugly. Nighttime became a lonelier place than ever: I tried to *get* it, to understand why Samson had done it, to find clues in my own experience of his bullying that might lead to the semblance of a conclusion. Make sense of it. Stop pretending what he did was okay. It wasn't. The difficult part was handling my own mood swings without his cushioning. Irresponsible and unpredictable as he might have been, Samson had at least been there to deal with me when I felt I was breaking down. Telling me to stop crying. Ordering me to the football pitch. Stroking my hair in what I'd thought was a fatherly way. He'd seen me in my little moments of insanity and tried to help. Now that I knew he, like me, had been caught in his private chasm, he didn't seem quite so scary. Just a lonely, drunken guy with too much patience one day and none whatever the next. Yet for this reason I now hated him, and couldn't explain to myself why.

He had featured, a couple of years before, in my humble

novel about the school shooting. I think — though I can't recall for certain, given the general blurriness of those days — that as a character in *Bride* his name had been Mr Cheswick. In the novel, he survived; or, more precisely, he did not even feature in the carnage at all. Somehow he just disappeared from the narrative, and never turned up again. And life had proved that, as in art, a man can just vanish without a warning and most people will never know the reasons. My real-life Mr Cheswick returned to me as some ghostly thing that filled me with bile and anger, and I wanted to rewrite things to make sense out of them. I wrote him an email but he never replied. He was gone. The school forgot about him, and the secret of his loathsomeness remained between a select few of us.

And that was too much to deal with. I felt as though the secret would become so important that I'd have to tell someone — and I knew that that would end up being my mother. But how to tell my mother? My Mr Cheswick had despised her, or at least found her grating. How much to tell her? I knew that by explaining what had happened would bring her illusions about my wonderful boarding school to a guttering death — the man she had apparently called (too often for his liking) to see if her son was doing well — the man who'd shown us around the campus on the day we went to visit the school for the first time — the man who'd told her I was a good kid and even a decent athlete when I put my heart into it — a drunken, cruel, tormented molester?

I mustn't tell her anything about it. Let her read the official explanation and let her believe it.

But by holding onto these thoughts, I felt myself imploding again. The chemicals in my head weren't right, if you listened to the doctors; but more than that, the abstract content of my thoughts wasn't right, wasn't rational. The world looked a smidgen less coherent than it had seemed already. One night it simply collapsed, and I was barely aware enough to know it until I found myself in hospital with my mother by my side.

EIGHT

Incoherent messages, little failed attempts at saying something to hide the big nothing, poured out of me the second time they put me in there — the hospital — this time in a room I no longer remember — a room like a pit I had dug for myself where I could rest but not for very long at all; it was hardly rest, if I stayed alive they would send me back out there eventually, out there but not with the same medication I'd grown used to — I was trying, failing and trying to express something inside of me that I couldn't quite understand, as though to dislodge some nugget of truth that had been caught in my veins — the real fear, as I knew but pretended not to know, was that the nugget was not there.

There is no nugget of truth. If there were, something, maybe not matter itself but surely something, would implode, most likely the thing harder than matter — words — would stop being useful in any way — because if some nugget of truth could be grasped what could would the various ways of expressing it be? But there is no nugget of truth and I was senselessly trying, senselessly failing — pulling out some fishbone in my throat that would finally, without any more conditions to be met, relieve me of this urge to communicate things I wasn't even aware of —

"do you know what I mean"

I asked this every time, and she would nod, my mother — nodding was her way of warding off the spirits that would do me harm — nodding away, telling me she was *listening*, if I wanted to speak she would listen, she'd stay put and hear my words even if they made no sense. And that was a problem, I wanted to have to *choose* my words — I did not want to be accepted as a matter of course — there ought to be no of course about it — I wanted to say something *very precise*, but I didn't know what it was:

"do you know what I mean"

and she'd nod and she had no idea, but she listened.

"do you know what I *mean* when I say I'm angry and not angry" I said

"I think so"

"what do I mean"

"I don't know, but I *think* I know, does that answer your question"

"maybe"

and she said:

"do *you* know what you mean"

and I said:

"no, I don't, I'm trying to tell you something but I don't even know what it is"

"find the words, I want to know"

"and I want to tell you, but expressing it is hard, it's weird"

"I know"

"I feel that there's a thing I'm hiding, but when I put it into words in my head it sounds wrong and false"

"you don't need to worry about the truth"

and I said:

"but I want some truth"

"there are more important things than speaking the truth"

"like what"

"like you getting better, my kiddie, like you being happy, like you being well again"

"I don't want to be well again, not if it's going to make me lose this urge"

"what urge"

"to tell the truth"

"you think you can't tell the truth when you're happy, then"

"I don't think I can"

"well that makes me very sad, you shouldn't think like that, even if it is true"

"but why are you pressuring me into changing"

"kiddie, I'm not pressuring you to do anything, to be anything, I just want you to feel happy, I worry so much about you"

"if you worry so much about me then why can't you help me figure it out"

"but figure what out"

"this, this problem, the problem of saying things"

"because I don't know any better than you do"

"and that's the real problem"

We sat in a room I don't remember — all I recall is yellow blinds yellowed further by the sun — and I was caught — couldn't ask to be taken home — stayed there for two weeks perhaps, two weeks in a room I paid no notice to — and when I wasn't asleep because of the drugs they pumped into me I was talking to my mother — trying to express something I couldn't express — all the while verging on admitting to myself that there was no nugget of truth — there was no final thing to say — no ultimate horizon of meaning — verging on it but never quite getting there — because if I let myself be taken by the current of nothingness that such a revelation might entail, who knew what would happen — could not kill myself — my mother would be destroyed — could not kill my mother — couldn't kill anything at all, nothing would be removed permanently — her space, my space would be taken up by something else — I wanted to remove the possibility of existing — to ensure it wouldn't happen again, any of this — and occasionally, when I wasn't saying these things to myself or to my mother, I hallucinated, saw repulsive giant spiders, eight of them, crawling out from beneath my pillow — they were *there* — they were enormous violent creatures, full of hatred — and just as quickly the hallucination was over and I was sound asleep —

"it's the drugs, they are giving you new medication in very big doses, it can make you see things that aren't there, but you don't have to worry, there's no danger, it's not for good, and you're safe here with me"

"but they were huge" I said

"I know, but they weren't real"

"but I saw them"

"I know"

How was I meant to get well with doctors pumping me full of drugs, stuff that made me see false monsters? My mother held my hand through the worst moments but this helped little — I was too enamored with this idea of there possibly being such a thing as truth — if I could only say a perfectly true sentence, these problems would disappear — but whatever the sentence — *I am unhappy* or *the sky is blue* or *the word DOG is a word* — it felt untrue, I was not always wholly miserable and the sky wasn't always blue and the word DOG was only a word by virtue of my having called it one — could there be a perfectly true sentence, and if so, could there be two, or three, a whole paragraph? Might I someday utter truth? No, not likely — but I wanted to try — it wouldn't work — but I must try — it would not work. And so I kept failing to say the simplest true thing, every word sounded hollow and counterfeit, I had borrowed everyone's words and if nobody knew how to say true things then there was no hope. Still I tried.

When the nurses brought me my food I ate it without interest — when they helped me to piss I pissed without relief — when they asked me how I was feeling I said I was fine because no other answer seemed appropriate — when they changed my sheets I was encouraged to walk around with the IV drip on wheels trailing by my side — the hospital smell never faded, I was always aware of it — sunlight outside — beautiful weather I was not allowed to enjoy — and after a week I gave up trying to say much and fell asleep for days on end — my mother kept me company the moments I was awake — and the conversation would continue:

"do you know what I mean"

"kiddie, I need you to explain everything, tell me"

"I don't even know what I want right now"

"what did you want before"

I told her I wanted some kind of meaning.

"I don't know anything about meaning" she said

"I see that"

"but don't you feel your life has any meaning at all"

"is meaning something you *feel*" I asked

and she said:

"my life has meaning because of you and your sister"

"is that all"

"it's more than enough"

"but that means your life depends on something else"

"so"

"doesn't it bother you that you can't just find some kind of meaning that isn't a *reason*, it's just a *thing* that stands alone and doesn't point to anything else"

"what do you mean"

"I don't even know"

"do you want some water"

"yes"

"I'll be right back"

and as my mother poured water into a paper cup someone knocked at the door and opened it, it was a young woman I had never met before, dressed like a professional of some sort, not a casual concerned visitor, but she had a friendly smile, and she said hello and she asked if she could come in and she came in, she placed some papers on a table and took a breath to convince herself she had a job to do and then she said:

"are you Philippe"

"yes"

"hello Philippe, my name is Teresa, I am a counselor, they may have mentioned that I was coming today"

"they didn't"

"they should have"

"they didn't"

"well, is this a good time"

and my mother said yes —

and Teresa looked at my mother and said:

"are you Philippe's mother"

"yes"

and Teresa introduced herself again and my mother shook her hand and Teresa sat at a chair and said:

"I understand it's been a difficult week for you"

"it's been a boring week"

she laughed uncomfortably and said:

"I can imagine"

and I said:

"there isn't much to do"

she said:

"I understand"

and my mother sat at my side and gave me the cup of water and I thanked her — then Teresa said:

"you know, the nurses tell me you're a wonderful patient, always polite"

her condescension was starting to grate but I said nothing because the nurses had said I was polite — and she said:

"I'm here to check up on you, see if you want to have a talk about anything, if you have things you'd like to discuss with me then I am here for you"

"thank you"

and she turned to my mother and said:

"might I ask you to leave me and Philippe alone for about twenty minutes"

and my mother nodded and grabbed her purse and said:

"I'll go for a walk"

and left the room after smiling at me.

Teresa wanted to know how I was doing. I said fine and she

said:

"I hope everyone's treating you well"

"yes"

"good, do you feel this has been restful"

"no"

"why not"

"because I'm in a hospital"

"there's no shame in that"

"I don't care about shame, I care about being in a hospital"

"I don't understand"

"I don't want to be here, does that really strike you as odd"

"but there's no shame in being here"

"I'm not talking about shame, I'm talking about the discomfort of being in a hospital, would you like some more details"

"details are good, tell me more"

I wanted to tell her there was nothing inherently good about details, there was nothing she could do to help me, that she was a patronizing, incompetent, bored looking idiot, and I remembered someone saying once that psychology was what you studied when you were not particularly good with people but you were not particularly good with machines, and I wanted to ask her about her job and turn the tables on her and be cruel, even merciless, but I didn't, and instead I said:

"what details do you want"

and she said:

"any that you feel like sharing:

"I don't feel like sharing anything"

"but you must have so much to say"

"why do you think that"

"because you've been under a lot of stress lately"

"stress, is that what you want to call it, stress is not the word"

"what is the word, then"

"the word is anger"

"what's making you angry"

"you are, for starters"

and she straightened up and said:

"why am I making you angry"

"because you are asking me question after question about how I feel without giving the slightest indication that you actually care"

"but I do care"

"and what makes you care"

"well"

"well what"

"are you angry because I'm here"

"no, I'm angry because you would rather be elsewhere and I would rather you didn't look so pissed off about doing what I presume to be your job"

and she didn't like this, I had stepped out of line, but by this point it was gushing out of me and I said:

"you know what makes me angrier than anything in the world right now, it's the fact that you find me insolent, you find me a spoiled little shit, that's what makes me angry, because I know you're neither as clever as you think nor as gifted as you think and you will never realize this, you'll never get it"

and she said "it's normal to be angry at your age"

"that has nothing to do with it"

"it does, young people often feel angry, I know you don't mean what you're saying"

"what a fine psychologist you are"

"what do you expect me to say to that"

"get the fuck out of here"

and she half-smiled and she pushed a button on the wall and I said:

"what are you doing"

and she said:

"I think I'll have to come back another time, when you're

feeling calmer"

and a nurse came in, a fat old woman I hadn't seen before, and Teresa said something to her that I couldn't hear. The nurse nodded and smiled at me. Then Teresa stood and said:

"I'm going to go outside"

and I said "good"

and she said:

"goodbye, I will come back another time..."

After Teresa was gone the old nurse checked my IV drip and replaced one of the bags on it. She wetted a towel and gave it to me and said you got agitated, it's all right, and I said:

"what a bitch"

and the old woman, not shocked by the language, said:

"that's what everyone says"

"really"

"yes, really, nobody likes that woman"

"then why don't they fire her"

"I'm sure I don't know the reason"

"well, she's a condescending bitch"

"some people just don't know how to talk to others"

and she patted me on the shoulder and left me alone, and I wondered if she meant me or Teresa.

When my mother returned she was slightly out of breath, but smiling, and she said hello my kiddie, and I told her about Teresa and I said I may have been out of line, but my mother said:

"don't worry"

so I didn't worry. We never heard from Teresa again, nor did we hear anyone say anything about her. It was as if she'd vanished. The old fat nurse was now forever present, changing my sheets, checking my IV drip, patting me on the shoulder — you poor boy — and when I left the hospital she gave me a hug.

Leaving was hard. The doctor, a short round man with a beard and suspiciously legible handwriting, asked me how I was feeling:

"fine"

"good, it's been a rough couple days for you"

"yes"

"but you feel stronger"

"somewhat"

"good, good" and he looked at me with strange eyes: "you are a brave one"

"thank you"

and I had no idea what was going on anymore. But the details of my life before the hospital were returning urgently, as though they couldn't stretch any farther away from me and needed to fly back and hit me in the face. No more hospital bed far away from the other students. No more speaking to my mother in cryptic near-messages. No more Teresa.

I had left school in the Alps with my mother in an emotional blizzard I could almost remember but not quite. The headmaster had assured us that I'd be most welcome back if I felt better later on in the term; my room would not be given to someone else. Samson was gone, fired. Rima I could barely remember. There had been that other substance in me, a fireball, sheer hatred directed at nobody that I could identify. The rage had kicked in sometime during the night, and I'd called my mother in Portugal, told her I couldn't take it —

so she said:

"what's wrong, kiddie"

"I don't know, I'm burning up"

"what do you mean, burning up"

"I don't know, I don't know, help me"

"but what happened"

"nothing, nothing, I don't know why I feel like this"

and she told me to go to bed, and after some kicking around I did, and the next day the rage was back as soon as I woke up. This all-consuming repulsive terrifying ugly thing growing inside me, this hatred that made no sense; I was almost sure I could kill someone, someone close to me. So my mother flew over and picked me up and took me to Portugal, made me leave everything as it was, my bed unmade, my clothes on the floor, she simply packed me a small suitcase and we drove to the airport in Geneva and took the next available plane back to Portugal.

NINE

How much did I know about my mother? How much time did I spend during her lifetime trying to understand who she was, not merely as a mother but as an insecure, conflicted, upright but frail human being?

I am looking through my mother's bookshelves. A few months ago, when I was last here, I scanned the titles and picked the books I thought would be interesting to read — nobody else is going to read them, so... — but now I am looking at every book carefully, checking for creases in the spines, notes in the margins, blocks of fluorescent yellow on the pages, anything to help me understand how her mind worked. My imagination is stirring up. Perhaps I will find a note somewhere, a little folded-up slip of paper hidden in one of the books. Probably the Russian grammar books; she had too many of those. The note will say: *I am not gone, kiddo, and you can find me if you really miss me.* A joke? A teasing from beyond the grave? Or is she really not gone — whatever it means to be gone... So I look at the note again and I notice a little scribble on the envelope — a single word: *One.* Is this the first of many notes?

Pore over every single book I can find. *Basics of Russian Grammar. Teach Yourself Russian. How to Have a Conversation in Russian.* And Pushkin, Lermontov, Gogol, Dostoevsky, Tolstoy. Then there are the recipe books, the Bible in French, the old textbooks she used when she was doing her PhD, before she dropped out to take better care of us. Open every book, flick through every page, until I find another note. But there is none. At once the house looks huge, greater than I've ever seen it. And more imposing, more austere, darker. I start again. Find that fucking note. I want to see number *Two.* An hour later and there's nothing to show for the wasted time. *I am not gone, kiddo, and you can find me if you really miss me.* Well — how I miss you!

Retreat to the kitchen, pour a glass of water. There's no point in pursuing this. I am dreaming. But if I'm not, then there is a chance that we can be reunited. Find you and hug you. I look — I rummage, check under the bed, open the picture frames and peek inside. Take out the cutlery and feel around in the drawers. The empty animal cages where we used to keep chinchillas, rabbits, tiny nameless birds, hamsters, squirrels. The pillow-cases, look inside those. I pick up the bottles of wine nobody ever drank and peel off their labels. Leaf through the stacks of envelopes that haven't been opened, bills and bills addressed to a dead woman, debts that have outlived my mom. Open them all. Inside the cereal boxes, inside the packs of tampons in the bathroom, inside the cardboard boxes in the basement where all my old junk has been stored.

Someone knocks at the door and my quest is interrupted. I rush up the stairs, but the door's already open. It's Vlad. The man who loved my mother. His eyes are still missing the spark they used to carry. He looks like a dead man. He's never learned to speak Portuguese with any kind of comfort, but he's always tried with me. And he says:

"I want to see if you okay"

and I tell him I'm fine

"you are sure, yes"

"I'm fine"

"but me I am not so fine"

"do you want to sit down"

"yes, we sit and talk, okay"

"sure"

and we take a seat at the kitchen table and he notices the mess I've been making. He says:

"what happen here"

"nothing, I've just been careless"

"why everything so messy"

"it doesn't matter, how are you"

"not so good, I feel not so good, I miss your mother"

"I know, so do I"

"she was good woman, so good woman"

"I know"

"when you say to me that she is dead, I cannot believe"

"I can't believe it either, it seems unfair"

"but she is dead and I am so alone"

"you're not alone"

But he is. She was the only thing that kept him going, the reason he'd found himself able to smile.

Vlad wants to get married, my mother told me once. And I said:

"are you going to say yes"

and she said:

"no, I don't think so"

"why not"

"because I can't get married again"

"why not"

"because marriage is a big commitment, and I love Vlad very much, but he wants to be a family, and I don't think it's the right time for that kind of change"

"will you ever consider it"

"I don't think so"

"but he's really nice, everyone likes him and he likes everyone"

"yes, but it's more complicated than that"

"complicated how"

"complicated"

"but how"

"it's difficult to explain, but I think it's just not right, it wouldn't be fair to him or to me"

"how can marriage not be *fair*"

"I don't want to marry him"

"you just don't"

"I just don't"

"but you love him"

"yes"

"and you want to stay with him"

"yes, I just don't want to get married"

Now, sitting with Vlad, I want to ask him things I should never ask. Whether my mother was faithful. Whether he depended on her, not only emotionally, but in matters more mundane than love: the money, the security. He is a poor Ukrainian immigrant earning his living as a jack of all trades, fixing things, building things, fixing them again. He is the sweetest man ever to have stayed in this house. And he loved my mother with the kind of destructive insecurity that will turn him into a shell now that she's gone. He loved everything about her, about her children, about me and my sister and the two dogs and the cats, all of us were her children, and Vlad managed to love us all. He carried her in his arms when she fell to the floor on the day she died, when she'd had that explosion in her brain. I will not forget those words: an explosion in the brain. He carried her in his arms to the car and drove her to the hospital and then the doctors shooed him away and he was left without any news until she was dead and I told him so. And that night we drank wine and he wept and I was too numb to weep.

After Vlad leaves I return to my mother's room and sit on her bed and think: where the hell is number *Two* and will I ever find it? But when I look for the first note, it's gone. I had placed it on the window sill and it isn't there anymore. Was it all a fantasy? I was dreaming, perhaps; on this very bed, even. Of course there's no chance of seeing her again. I know exactly where she is. She is buried in a plot of land in the countryside next to other forgotten people. But being here reminds me of another time, back when she was alive and kind and wonderful.

We sat in this room one night. That was unusual enough. This room was her private world and I rarely entered it. We were alone, Vlad had gone for a drink with his childhood friend, my sister was with her group of girlfriends, and the dogs had been fed and wanted nothing from us anymore. My mother and I sat on the bed and that felt awkward, so I stood and paced around the room and she remained on the bed.

I was twenty years old and in my first year of university. I had fallen in love with a girl who ended up proposing to me, and who later withdrew the proposal. Now I was trying to forget her. The shock of seeing her love torn out of me had sent me on another pleasant spiral downwards. Eventually it got unbearable and my mother flew to England to make me speak to a few doctors. They decided it was time to change my medication. So for ten days I stayed at private clinic, where they could control the levels in my blood, and other factors. And so now I was out of there and in Portugal again with my mother during a term break.

I paced. For years I had paced — as I write this I am taking small breaks to pace and decide which details to leave out — and for years more I hope to pace. She sat placid as ever on the edge of her bed and looked at me and shook her head and said:

"you're pacing a lot these days, do you still feel anxious"

and I said:

"yes"

so she said:

"maybe you should take some lorazepam"

"I have"

"then do some stretches"

"I have"

"okay, then I guess you're happy just pacing around"

"pretty much, I don't trust anyone who doesn't pace when they're thinking, it means they body's not in sync with their mind"

Lorazepam, a drug I had been prescribed for my anxiety, had become a way of life for me. I enjoyed watching five or six pills dissolving in a bottle of flavored water, shaking the bottle, then taking sips throughout the day. It wasn't the healthiest thing to do, but I suppose by that stage I was hooked on the stuff. I called it birdseed instead of lorazepam: if the great nightbird of depression wanted its birdseed, then I would eat it instead. And then there would be no feeding the depression, and the anxiety drifted off into some layer of my mind to which I had no access. My muscles relaxed. My mind focused. I stopped sweating, and though the pacing never stopped, it didn't bother me at all. I'd been taking birdseed since high school, and it was an addictive thing — but at least it helped me function like a young adult instead of a scared chinchilla. I was careful not to let my mother know just how much of it I took. So when she suggested that I take birdseed that night, I neglected to tell her I'd already taken more than she would have liked me to take.

So I paced and we spoke of things I had been reading, that she had been reading. From the age of nineteen I had developed an almost obsessive interest in psychoanalysis; I'd read seven or eight texts by Freud while I was at the clinic after my fiancée had disappeared from my realm of tangible things. Something about Freud's style bothered me — it was clean, clear and accessible; his arguments were developed in ways I could follow; but this ease of entrance into the Freudian world (though that world seemed occasionally inconsistent and contradictory) perturbed me more than the revelations contained therein. If this stuff, all these strange insights into how human subjectivity might work, could be explained in prose that was digestible, maybe even *easy*, how could it be valid? How could all these complicated twists and knots that made up the human psyche be reduced to a mostly coherent set of essays and case studies? How was I supposed to feel to have my unconscious — which I had just been given as a gift by reading my first page of Freud — explained to me about as well as it could be by Freud; and this, despite his protestations, his insistence that he could not fully explain away the unconscious? If the unconscious was a deep dark mystery, and at night I dipped into it in my dreams — or perhaps it dipped into *me,* the space I called *me* — then I did not want the mystery made less mysterious. Yet Freud was good at showing what was going on, and even his kookier pronouncements carried with them an authority that I couldn't deny.

My mother was privy to my thoughts on psychoanalysis. She was unconvinced by the whole thing, but at least it wasn't *Lacan,* she said. It happened that not long after my twentieth birthday I began a quest to *understand* Lacan, that most difficult and obscure of Freud's followers. Where Freud was palatable and even enjoyable as a stylist, Lacan's prose was less prose than games of encryption and elliptical evasions. I could read Lacan for ten minutes at a time and fail to understand anything I'd just read — and that was the challenge: to grasp the Lacanian secret, to crack the weird codes in his texts and figure out if it made sense at all. I ordered five, six, then eight or nine introductions to Lacanian psychoanalysis and I read them with a pencil in my hand to underline anything that might help get something out of it. Then I'd speak to my mother about my reading. She remained skeptical, but she heard me out, and didn't raise an eyebrow when I spoke of the object-cause of desire, the symbolic, the topology of the subject:

"what the heck do *you* know about topology" she said

"I'm not sure, I want you to explain it to me"

"it's very complicated"

"well try; *you* were a mathematics professor, not me"

and she'd explain it to me in the simplest language she could find, and I'd say:

"oh, okay"

and she'd say:

"I don't quite see what that's got to do with subjectivity"

"me neither"

That night, having taken my birdseed and read my fill of Lacan without really grasping much, I paced around my mother's room and spoke at length about the Lacanian phallus, the *name of desire*, the *signifier of lack*... she said:

"why do these intellectuals always insist there's something *lacking* in people"

and I gave her a standard Lacanian answer, which she ignored, so I said:

"don't you feel there's a lack inside you"

"no, if anything I feel there's too much, there's an abundance of unnecessary things in human beings"

"like what"

"like feelings that get in the way of stuff"

"like what"

"like, oh, I don't know, kiddie, like changes in moods, why must moods change, if good feelings didn't have to turn bad life would be so much more wonderful"

"but you see, that's not going to happen and the fact that you wish for these things indicates a lack in you"

"oh, blah-blah with your lack"

"but it's true"

"it may be true but what are you going to do about it, if there's a lack in you that constitutes you as a subject, as you put it, then what exactly can you do about it"

"nothing"

"there you go"

and I said:

"but it's interesting to think about it"

"I'm sure it is, and if it helps you understand yourself then it's also useful, but I think there is more to life than Freud and Lacan"

"I know that"

"sometimes I wonder if you do"

The dogs sauntered into the room and sat by the bed. My mother patted one on the head: hello, sweet puppies. I stopped my pacing and looked at her shelf. Most of the books she kept in her room were those teach-yourself-Russian textbooks. She had taught herself to speak fluent Russian over a matter of four or five years. She could only communicate with Vlad in Russian. Her prowess for languages was astounding, but back then I paid little attention to it. That night was the first time I seriously wondered why she would want to learn Russian when she knew so few Russian-speakers. I said:

"why did you learn Russian"

and she looked at me and smiled and said:

"it's fun to learn languages"

"yes but I've seen you lying on the couch for hours learning the grammar and the little details and that's a lot of work"

"if you want to learn a language you have to learn it properly"

"but why Russian"

"because it's a beautiful language"

"you didn't know that when you were starting out, you couldn't have known, so why"

"because, kiddie, it's fun"

She stroked the dogs and sighed. I didn't often doubt that she was telling the truth, but that night I pushed harder. The element of weirdness present in everyone was well concealed in her, so I had to look a little more carefully to discover it. People have unusual motivations for things; what had been her reason for learning a language from scratch, a language as complicated and alien to us as Russian? But she refused to tell me any more than that.

"you won't believe me, but sometimes it helps with the stress to lie down and learn grammar"

"that sounds awfully boring"

"you can talk, Mr Lacan"

"at least there is substance in Lacan"

"I'm sure"

and she carried on stroking the dogs, one with each hand, until they were stretching out their hind legs and making grunting pleasure-sounds.

I was in an inquisitive mood. I wanted to know my mother: to know who she was when she wasn't being a parent. I would accept any details, so long as there were details to be shared that night. And so I pressed on:

"why *Russian* though"

"oh kiddie, you ask so many questions"

"but you never answer them"

"I liked the *sound* of the language, the words, the way the words sound when you say them properly"

"that's crap, tell me the truth"

"you seem to think that's not the whole story"

"of course I don't think it's the whole story, I want to know what you are hiding from me"

"maybe someday"

"no, not this again, you always say that *someday* you'll tell me about some big secret"

"and someday I will"

"no, you should tell me now"

"I can't tell you now"

"why"

"because I have sworn not to tell and it involves other people that you know"

"like who"

"it doesn't matter"

"it does"

"child, why are you so desperate to know this"

"because it's mysterious"

"that it is"

and she smiled and I said:

"please tell me"

"I can't"

"tell me at least what it's *about*"

"nope"

"please"

"nope"

"but *why*"

"because it involves *other people,* kiddo"

Onwards I plowed, insisting and begging and being a genuine brat about it.

"is it about our family"

"nope"

"is it about *you*"

"yes, of course it's about me"

"who else"

"I shouldn't even have said anything about this" she said, and she sighed

"yes you should have, and you should tell me more"

"but I can't"

and eventually she told me. But she gave me the barest details, the most infuriatingly cryptic summary of her secret life; she told me her secret in a resigned voice, still stroking the dogs, while I paced and frowned and listened to her half-story, the story of her life as a spy.

A spy; nothing quite as glamorous as James Bond, she insisted, but something of the sort. A spy — a *spy?* Whom did she spy *on?* Why? When? My pacing turned into a kind of jogging in place. A spy for whom? The United Kingdom, she said. What? But she wasn't even British. No, she wasn't — but you know that good friend of hers, Mister S—, with whom she so often dined and went to embassy galas? That Mister S—, charming Englishman, Oxbridge-bred, recently divorced, yes, that Mister S— worked for the British government. That's ridiculous. Not so ridiculous as all that. He had been a spy himself once, but he'd been found out. Now he hired other people. It's that simple? It is when nobody suspects you of doing it. And you know all those books about Russian grammar? Those were the books she had used to master the Russian language. But for what? Why, for her espionage work. She was *spying* on the *Russians?* Nothing dangerous, don't worry. But yes, sometimes, as a favor to Mr S—, she got friendly with certain visiting Russian politicians and... and what? What did she do? She tried to extract information from them. After gaining their confidence. But that's insane! Well, she didn't do it often. She was not *employed* by MI5. She did little jobs for Mr S—, and that was that. So she wasn't even paid? No. Of course not. If she had accepted money for it, life would have been far, far more complicated. As it stood, she was simply useful to a retired spy who still had some status in the British intelligence agencies. She spoke Russian — how many Portuguese citizens do you know who speak English, Portuguese, French *and* Russian absolutely fluently? But when did all this take place? Oh, years ago. When you were around fifteen.

Fifteen — I was fifteen years old, just getting over Rima, dragging my mother into my psychotic breakdowns, screaming, wrecking things, crying for no reason, hurling insults at everyone, despising myself — fifteen, by which point I'd already seen the doctor in Switzerland and been prescribed medication — while I was fifteen years old and falling apart, my mother had found the unlikeliest way of distracting herself imaginable — spying on Russian politicians. Was it all a joke? Was she serious? She was dead serious. My mother had never been a good liar. And I hadn't known her to play a practical joke on anybody. Not a single one. She told me these things and she would not give me the exact details — *yet.*

"one day when you are older and Mr S— has moved back to the UK and enough time has passed, I will tell you the rest"

"do you promise"

"I swear it, kiddo"

"you aren't lying, are you"

"I swear it's the truth"

Was she mad? Had she placed our family in danger for years

— the fact that she had refused payment for her activities didn't really soothe me — for years — for years? And now she wanted me to promise never to tell my sister — you know how your sister has so many friends, I don't want her to tell her friends, you understand, she's too young for this kind of thing — for years! For years, during that deep and terrible depression I was struggling to climb out of, my mother, my mommy, was going to the Russian embassy-hosted galas and possibly bedding Mr Russian Politician just to get information — no, probably not that far, probably it was just gaining their trust but — but what if she had whored herself out to acquire sensitive data — what if —the possibilities, endless and all repulsive, coursed through my head that night, after my mother had gone to bed — *was she lying?* Well, was she?

But the details added up. There had always been something mysterious about Mr S—, that refined old man with the impeccable manners, who seemed to know something about absolutely everything. The way he called her in the middle of meals and she had to excuse herself and speak to him for twenty minutes at a time; the way my mother... no. The more I thought about it, the less I *wanted* to think about it. I went to sleep with so many questions in my head that I resolved to get to the bottom of things once and for all.

The next morning, however, she refused to speak of it. In fact, for the next year she wouldn't even acknowledge the conversation we'd had. And by the end of that year, she was dead. I know nothing more. I can tell you nothing more.

TEN

But I can imagine. Sure enough, as time passes and I find myself caught up in new dramas, friendships and mysteries, the memory of that night in my mother's bedroom takes on ever greater proportions — that is the part of her I knew the least, the most surprising aspect of an endless woman now dead but guttering in the back of my mind. When I sit at a coffee shop on my own with a notepad open in front of me, I wonder: what was my mother doing when *spying* or whatever you wish to call it? Whom did she spy on? What could have led her to engage in these stupid activities? And into the notepad go the observations I make of hypothetical Russians, men important enough to warrant a need for espionage in any amount, men I've never met but whose lives crossed my mother's at some time I will never be able to pin down.

One man stands out above the others. A typical, easy but elaborate fabrication: a Russian playboy, the kind of man you'd expect any woman to feel attracted to — and to deny her attraction, because nobody will admit to *wanting* such a man, such a heartless conqueror. In this fantasy, my mother is asked to spy on him because nobody knows what he's been up to. He doesn't seem dangerous, not exactly that, and he's not so high profile that you'd hire a professional to spy on him; he's just enough of a character for someone, for Mr S—, to ask a little lady like my mother, bored or desperately looking for a distraction from the turbulence of her family life, to get close to Mr Playboy and find out just what he's up to, why he's in Portugal at this very moment, what he thinks of this or that, all these menial but maybe significant details. And I feel compelled to imagine him all the way out of my dreams and into what we call reality.

He is a fiend, a charmer, an incomparable seducer. Pride of the family. Never let his parents down. They could depend on him, they knew who he'd turn out to be. A charmer, a seducer with a conscience, a reliable, happy man. Now they're gone, long dead or senile, he doesn't check anymore, and he's filled out his suits with muscles. Always with the suits, some dark shade of brown, which is not what diplomats wear, but he makes that okay, acceptable. Wears a tie in the middle of the afternoon on a Sunday. Forever wearing a tie, because that makes you look trustworthy; after a while you trust yourself more when there's a tie around your neck. His father never wore a tie in his life. When they buried him they put him in a suit without a tie. Something about it being like a noose, and he hated that, had a rabid fear of being choked to death.

This fiend walks with a tiny limp, you wouldn't notice unless you paid attention, a relic of his younger days when he fought. He used to kick things, people, punched them and they punched him back. This, his parents never knew. He avoided black eyes, bruises; he was too quick. When he was fighting in the back alleys with his comrades, they were all comrades back then, he'd win every time. But that didn't discourage his foes. They wanted to beat him, take his ear as a trophy. So every few weeks there'd be a fight, a few mean, stupid, broken-looking thug-idiots he called semi-friends, gathering around him and saying, take your pick, and they meant it. And he always won. Landed punches in the right places, left them gasping, writhing, gurgling, saying you fucking genius, almost genuine when they laughed and could not believe he'd beaten them again, until it had become a bond, and they went from semi-friends to real friends. Those thuggish young men with missing teeth and shaved heads, living in the darkest crevasses hidden somewhere in Moscow, had found a leader. His name was Piotr something, he didn't want his name going around, but yes, that was him, he was the guy, the charmer, so good to his parents, the cruel ruthless mighty warrior of the streets, leading a small group of idiots with no hope and no ambition. No hope and no ambition but still a burning and horrible urge to feel something, to have done things by the time all their teeth were gone. These guys were brutal, but they were little boys, and they needed guidance, and Piotr, once the fighting was over, once they knew he could teach them how to fight dirtier than they had ever fought, this Piotr could be the key to some kind of meaning.

But that was on the side, at least at first. Piotr kept himself busy being a model young man. Got the grades he needed to study literature at the university. Read everything he was asked to read, found himself bored by most of it. Literature, like most things, was an ornament in his personality, something to keep the mask clean and attractive. What he craved was action: the fighting, the violence of those back alleys. But literature gave him a smoothed out surface on the outside. He could quote Pushkin but also the great American writers, whose books he kept smuggled copies of under his bed. And he read Zola, and Keats, and the spectrum that kept these two apart. He read and read, but rarely enjoyed any of it on a gut level. It was all enrichment, a way of seeing how these more intelligent men had said the things he would later say to women, to professors, and, eventually, to other politicians, to my mother. The more he read, the more he could pretend to understand — having by now given up the task of grasping the real, the *here*, the condition we find ourselves in — he could pretend at least to understand, and to formulate things in a way that might seem enlightening to his listeners. He read because he wanted to speak and be heard.

And he managed: by the time he'd started his degree in economics, *a most unusual change of careers* and one typically forbidden by the state university, by the time he'd started delving into unpredictable matters (it was unpredictable, and he and his professors secretly knew this, there is no predicting the numbers) and almost fascinating, everything soaked through with a nauseating, moribund Soviet sanctimoniousness, by that time he was a young man of some influence on the streets. Not a crook, exactly. And certainly he spent less and less time out there, and the fighting had stopped, his disciples having all but desisted now that he was bigger than they were from the hours he lifted weights; nevertheless there remained in his thoughts a subversive wish to dominate and destroy. The thugs at his side were perfect pawns for this. He would not dabble in the criminal. But flirting with it, always pushing, treading closer and closer to the line of the unacceptable, became his hobby, his little project. After his academic duties, he and his comrades, whom he had subdued in the eyes of the law, and converted into placid civilians working in factories and only getting drunk at appropriate times, would sit and drink and touch women in various ways, most of them welcome, and he would declare his desire to enter politics. And his comrades said this looked very likely, very possible. Indeed it was. In power, he might be differently entertained, no longer stuck impressing these morons for no real gain except easy access to women. In power, he would be known as a reformer, a real leader. He could do it. People are malleable and they are begging to be led. If our silly obsession with communism would only *die*. If we could only be Western, and free to be afraid without the threat of a whip.

He was thirty when the wall fell. A still-young man finishing his doctoral studies, father to two girls he took exceptional pains to be a daddy around. Twins, and the mother, whom he'd married because of a not entirely conscious stratagem, was called Elena. He was endlessly unfaithful, and she, being weak, endlessly forgave him. He never hit her. He had not hit anybody in years. No fights. Now his thugs were more polished, almost respectable fools. When the temptation for profit — a great, terrible temptation — arose and the Russian mafiosi started to grow in numbers, profiting a little too easily from the collapse of the Soviet Union, and were looking for trustworthy bodyguards, Piotr kept his brutes sober. None of this, he said. We are not mobsters, and we will never be mobsters. I know what I'm up against. Now's the time to get into the dumb game of politics. Become a public presence. Work my way up.

And he did. He launched a company and left it in the hands of one of his smarter brutes. The business thrived, made the news. But it was never on Piotr's mind. What mattered was gaining all the credibility he could find. He had a PhD; he ran a successful business venture; he was respectably married, a family man; his record was clean; and more importantly, he had connections. These he had found in various places, probing here and there until something looked promising. He'd befriended the talents in his city. He'd traveled. And he was a charmer, a seducer —trustworthy-seeming, firm of handshake, good looking enough, always in those brown suits with a tie wrapped neatly around his neck.

It promised to be a career: new businesses, new friendships or alliances or tense combinations thereof; another child, this time a boy; he spoke in public, appeared on television, on the radio, made money. They called him Brown Bear, a true patriot in a brown suit. But he entered no campaigns, and as the years passed he took smaller and smaller roles in political events. He sold his businesses. For months at a time he disappeared. Elena declined to speak of his whereabouts. The children knew better than to ask. Piotr Popov, Brown Bear, seemed to retreat into the darkness for increasingly long bouts of... what? Orgies? Espionage-related nonsense? The man simply vanished one day, and reappeared four months later, refusing to answer questions about anything, neither confirming nor denying the rumors that he and Elena were agreeing on a divorce settlement, resolutely mumbling *no comment* whenever a reporter caught him out in the streets.

Brown Bear Popov, the once-promising political aspirant, no longer cared. And to this day he remains indifferent to politics, to power, to his former thuggish friends, who would have made such powerful bodyguards. It is 2003, and Piotr, still a charmer, still popular with women, simply doesn't give a fuck anymore. The world is beginning to forget him. It forgets things quickly, but he was a personality, so full of potential. Nobody *wants* to forget him. So he flies off to Gibraltar or, why not, to Fiji, to the Seychelles, and, with his woman, whoever she is this time, he sits and stares at the ocean and thinks. Even he has trouble understanding it. The point at which he stopped caring. It happened gradually, but not quite slowly. Maybe a period of four months. The attachments he'd formed to things dissolved. His wife bored him more than ever; his children felt to him *not his*, not a part of his life, not interesting or interested in him. It was as though everything he'd worked to build throughout his life, through the collapse of Sovietism to the crisis of 9/11, through so many pointless discussions with his tearful wife, through so much boring talk with other political hopefuls, so much nonsensical jabbering on the radio, so many empty women willing to share his bed, so much God damned everyday stupid *bullshit,* everything had suddenly lost any shred of meaning it had once appeared to contain. The universe cracked open ever so slightly, but he saw it — he saw through the crack to a blinding light that left him dazed, blinded, bitter, disillusioned. Nothing was the same after he woke up on that little nameless island next to that little nameless woman whose uncovered breasts quivered with the breaths she took in her sleep and he understood, once and for all, that he had stopped caring about anything. The world was exactly as a part of him had suspected all along — aimless, lost and so vain, so ugly and vain.

No liberation. He has thrown off the shackles but he isn't free. It is 2003 and Piotr is lying in his bed in a hotel on the coast of Madeira. He is alone. Last night he hired his first, his last, prostitute. Everything went exactly as he had expected: the sex act itself felt like nothing more than an extension of his world view. She sucked his cock. Then he did the deed for a few minutes, got bored, and stopped. He looked at her, looking back at him with bored and condescending eyes, and sighed.

"what's the matter" she said

"nothing"

"aren't you having fun, handsome"

"I'm fine, I'm done"

"but you didn't come, baby"

"get out of here"

and she shrugged. She dressed, looked at him a little strangely, and left. He sat on the bed and thought. What did he think about? He can't even remember. It was not about the whore. No guilt, nothing like that. He sat and thought about things he can't remember, and then he woke up hours later right here. He's tired, his muscles ache. He didn't come. He paid a woman to fuck him — and he didn't come. It's not even embarrassing; it's a sign. He's going to see fewer and fewer people as time goes by. Soon he'll give up even women. He's sick of their smell, their skin, their lipstick. Lipstick traces on his clothes will be a thing of the past. Give up everything.

He knows, from the books, from his studies, his youth buried in Goethe and *The Anatomy of Melancholy* and *Paris Spleen* so many others, he knows what he's going through. Today we would call it a depression. But it isn't that. He isn't sad, though his misery is becoming more pronounced daily. It's as if every action of his, the smallest and most inconsequential, finds a way to rock the boat a little harder and threatens to cast him into the black ocean. No — in fact it does not have to be black. It is clear, so perfectly clear; he is drowning in realism, he is seeing everything for the vanity of vanities that we, as a species, as a chemical curiosity, have discovered all of this to be. He is not depressed, he is aware, he's *looking* and *noticing* that nothing has any worth, and that even under such conditions, the only conditions, it is possible to continue to live.

And this is why, tomorrow, he will fly back to Portugal, and from there, a few days later, to Berlin, and from Berlin back to

Russia. Not Moscow; not yet. He doesn't want to be seen again so soon. He only left a few weeks ago. And the Russians are losing hope in a very different way; he won't mingle with that kind of despair. He'll fly to some little village somewhere rural, a place neither hot nor cold. And he'll stay there for a bit, breathe the Russian countryside air, read, whatever. Stay away from people. He spends the day lying in bed wondering about very little, but wondering. A mild impulse of curiosity toward deciphering the textures on the walls, the ceiling, his skin. As though there were a code to crack yet. To keep him busy. And to keep him afloat. Various times he gets up to write down thoughts on the notepad provided by the hotel. He remembers, in particular, out of no context that he can figure out, the words his father spoke once years ago. *Never claim to have won. Never tell anyone you are the victor. Future generations will mock you for it.* Why is he thinking about this now? It doesn't matter. He is free to roam the intellectual fields. He scribbles those words down as accurately as he can remember, which is not very. Then he lies back down in bed and thinks it through, thinks the little aphorism out. Future generations will mock you for it. Wise words for those who still consider time a friend. But time is neither friend nor foe. Time is nothing, nothingness in flux, the necessary emptiness that allows the world to move one atom after another. That's all. And Piotr has given up even trying to understand its nature; he's happy just to see the emptiness for what it seems to be.

But time does tease. It strokes your crotch and leaves you looking to the future. It creaks like a forgotten staircase when you aren't paying attention and makes you jump. Sometimes it threatens to end, and then it expands like a once-folded blanket and leaves you to sigh out your relief. These things, these qualities of time, not-friend and not-foe, make Piotr think himself into a funk. Suddenly it isn't so clear that he is seeing things as they are. No explaining it, of course. But now he's placed everything in doubt, without having tried to, and by the time he's fully alert again he is quivering from the cold and the sun is setting and he needs to piss from the cock that couldn't come last night. When he gets to Lisbon tomorrow, he will not hire another hooker. That was a stupid thing to have done. He'll sleep. As he is about to sleep now.

Mother, I can't link you to this man. What do you have in common with him? What good could he have been to you, who were so rarely prey to men like him? Yet something happened — you engaged in some sort of affair with him. I have no proof, but my mind has wandered so far in this direction that nothing persuades me otherwise. You grew bored with the monotony of everyday bullshit. You lived to care for me, for my sister, for the family. Feeding and cleaning and walking the dogs that had continued to need walking long after I'd left you for my life in Switzerland. Putting up with so many dull household chores. You didn't have a job anymore. The house was a constant battle-field, where decay and time tried to destroy the life you'd built. The cats clawing at the furniture, the chinchillas rolling around in their sandy cages, the maid yawning and not doing quite as much work as you paid her to do, the phone calls from hysterical relatives, the fungus growing on the walls because of that stupid dampness problem nobody had warned you about when you bought the house, and more phone calls, and the dogs needing to be walked again, and your son off in another country maybe suffering but keeping quiet about his pain and you could only suspect, worry, probe gently so he wouldn't lose his temper — you needed a break and you took the first opportunity you could find.

That friendly Mr S—, whom you knew to be a former spy. Outed some years ago. Now working as a recruiter, perhaps? Is that what it was? He was in Portugal because the British government had found a use for him there, is that it? And he became a friend of yours, a good conversation partner, a charming old man. Seemed to know something about everything. Had lived a life of danger. And one day he approached *you*, the single parent of two lovely but exhausting teenagers, whom you loved but needed a break from, and asked if you'd be interested in doing him a favor. A small favor, but also a big favor. You see, I'm going to be honest with you. I need somebody who can speak Russian, and whom I can trust. There aren't many people like that around here. And I do trust you, Sophia. I trust you very much and I wouldn't ask if I didn't hold this much trust in you. The thing is, well, there is a man, a former politician, a Russian. A guy who once seemed to be very important, an up-and- comer, even had a nickname, Brown Bear, because he always wore brown suits in public. A former friend of Putin's, I'm told. Like any Russian official, Brown Bear, well, he's shady. Nobody quite knows what's up with him, what he's doing, and what he happens to be doing here in Lisbon. He's been here for two days. The curious thing is that he seems to be alone, and this is the first time in forever that he's been spotted in public. You see, he quit politics a while back and has been popping up in different places around the world, he's been noticed quietly in the oddest places, never actually *doing* anything but... but somehow always intriguing his observers. Now, I shouldn't have an interest in this man at all. He's a nobody these days, not, as far as I know, politically active at all, though I couldn't tell you why he decided to call it quits when his career was on the rise. Well, that's irrelevant. The key thing is that I *am* interested in him. There are, um, several things that I want to know about him. I don't quite know how to explain.

ELEVEN

... and I *was* an intellectual once, you know. You may not believe me now but once upon a time there was nothing I wouldn't read. I was good friends with my teachers in school, because I was a dedicated student and always behaved correctly. I know you can't see me like that because I'm just your silly mother to you, but back when I had more free time, that is, when I wasn't raising you and your sister every single day, when I was allowed to spend a couple of hours at the library whenever I wished, well, *back then* I was a normal teenage girl like any other, except that I got married when I was nineteen and had to grow up fast. But the years before that, when I had just met your father and I had every reason to be alive, and he and I could talk about philosophy and books for hours on end, those were years where I made the most of myself and my life. Oh, yes, laugh away, but you'll see that you, too, will one day have to put the books down and make something of yourself...

... and I think I told you this, tell me if I have, but there was a time when I was a little girl when I went swimming in a lake and made friends with a frog. A tiny, slimy green thing that followed me around wherever I swam, as though it truly wanted to be my friend, a permanent companion, like it could read my thoughts and knew my loneliness. I'd swim to one end of the lake and it would follow me, and then to the other side, and it was still right behind me. Then I let it walk onto my shoulder and it remained there for at least a few minutes, totally unworried, because we were friends...

... about the same time that her little brother got cancer, your mother shut herself up into her own world and wouldn't let me in. She was *so worried*, so devastated, so shocked into disbelief about the whole thing... and don't get me wrong, because it was hard for everybody, but your mother, well, she wasn't the same person afterwards. And I think she sometimes resented me for trying to help her feel better. It didn't matter how little I trod on her toes; it still aggravated her. I seemed to make things worse no matter how I handled things, and by the time of our divorce, after your uncle had recovered and everything *should* have got back to normal, nothing was the same and we realized we were only staying together for you and your sister...

... so by age twenty-three I was no longer on very good terms with your father, and we tried to work things out in our own way, but we'd quickly understood that each of us felt betrayed by *something* in the air, something between us that just didn't work anymore. Your father began to spend more time in his study, reading, writing, whatever it was he was doing, and I felt a little abandoned...

... your mother, you have to get this, your mother was an incredibly smart woman, and she was pretty, and she was funny, so on the one hand I felt like I was losing everything. But on the other hand it was agonizing to remain together like this. We couldn't talk, we couldn't get along. Each of us felt increasingly annoyed by the other, and we each found ways to cope...

... and eventually we had you, and a couple of years later we had your sister; for a while it was nice, everything was nice again, and I really thought that maybe, *maybe* your arrival had patched things up between me and your father, but that proved to be an illusion. There should be a law against having kids to save a marriage... not that we did that, of course not, that wasn't why, but *after* the fact it seemed that our marriage was officially broken and deep down I blamed myself as much as I did your father, since I'd decided to go through with having you *and then* having your sister, when I *knew* things weren't going very well in the house, but, well, that was what happened and there wasn't anything I could do to change things now. Your father was stricter than I was and he often thought I was too lenient, too indulgent when I took care of you. And of course that irritated me and left me exasperated, but I tried to listen to his advice and I did this because he liked this and I didn't do *that* because he didn't like that. He wasn't tyrannical at all, that isn't what I mean, he was simply hard for me to deal with. You know, we did a personality test once, quite early on, to see if the magazine we were reading could accurately describe our personalities, and my score indicated that I was about as liberal as I could be and your father was as conservative as anyone could be. No, I don't mean conservative like the neocons in America, I mean the real conservatives, with values and a Catholic upbringing and many good qualities, as you understand, but still extremely conservative, maybe even old-fashioned. You say he's become much more liberal now, which is interesting, because I can't see what might have changed to allow *that* to happen…

… one time your father was so angry he kicked a door down and broke it into pieces…

… your mother was terrific in many ways, but I couldn't understand her, she wouldn't let me in. I really think it happened when her little brother got ill. That was when it all changed. She was unrecognizable. Still smart, still friendly and everything else, but colder, quieter, sadder… I often felt like something was missing in our marriage that had once been there, and I never figured it out…

… oh, you think I'm just a boring old hag. But I'm telling you, kiddo, I've had my share of adventures in my life. I will tell you about them someday. No, not now. Right now there are still people who wouldn't want me to tell you…

… no, I am *not* going to tell you yet. Because it involves certain people whom you know…

… stop asking me! You've been asking for months, and I haven't given in, have I? No, because…

… do you promise not to tell anyone yet? I mean it, don't tell *anybody*, not even your sister, because she has lots of friends and I wouldn't want her to tell them? I mean, will you keep this a secret between us for *now*, until you're twenty-five or so and everyone involved has nothing to worry about anymore? Well, do you? You do. I'm trusting you with this... you know how I've been teaching myself Russian for so many years...

... and I was never officially paid by them, because I didn't want to put us in danger. But I did do little things for them. For instance, they wanted me to get close to an important Russian man, himself a suspected secret agent, and find out...

... you don't have to worry. Nobody is going to come after us. That's why I never accepted *any* form of payment from the British government. Of *course* it was dangerous, kiddo. That's *why* I didn't allow them to...

... oh, you think I'm kidding. You think I'm making this up to appease you. Good for you, child. You think I'm still hiding the truth from you. My adventures, my *so-called* adventures. Well, have it your way. I'm not going to insist that you believe me, but I do expect you to keep your promise and tell nobody. Not a single person...

... well, it started because of all those embassy balls and galas that I attended. I knew everyone, and everyone knew me, because I could speak French and English, Portuguese and Russian...

... it was about five years ago...

TWELVE

Dear everybody who knew my mother: please stop pitying the children. They are not dying and they are not in danger. The children are surviving and that is what my mother would have wanted so stop pitying the children.

Dear everybody who loved my mother: I know. It's sad and it's a tragedy and she was oh so young. The world has lost one of its finest angels. I know that you treasured her and you hope she is in a better place. I know, so please stop saying it.

Dear every doctor who treated my mother: some of you did a better job than others. Nobody but one could determine why she so often choked on water and on food and on the air itself. Why did my mother have those throat spasms? Why did she always complain of a dryness of the mouth? Aren't you doctors? If so, why did you not ever figure it out? What was wrong with her throat? Do you know that for years I entertained the nightmarish fantasy that she would choke to death for no good reason in the middle of a family meal? Sophia, Sophia, why did you choke so much? Was there sand in your throat? No spasms for a few days — that was good at first, but then it was for a few weeks, then you began to forget about the choking... the choking came back and again you were going to doctors, to America, to London, wherever help could be found. You would call me and say: the doctors think they may know what it is, it's my anemia, it's my muscles, it's my spine, it's my arm, it's my nerves, it's stress. These were your ailments. The anemia never went away no matter how many iron supplements you took. You complained of fatigue and you went to bed at four in the afternoon. You never ate meat so you never got better. Your muscles hurt and you didn't know why. Your spine was collapsing on itself, crushing a nerve in the process and that made your arm hurt. And because your arm hurt you couldn't drive so Vlad drove you everywhere.

And because you were anemic and you were afraid of eating because of the choking, and because your arm hurt and you had a bad back, and because none of the symptoms seemed to lessen, you were almost a cripple and demands were made of you that made you feel like a cripple. Where were your doctors and what were they doing with your money? Dear doctors, why couldn't you help my mother? Was it impossible or was it expensive or was it just too much work? I forgive you. You are not me and you have not lost my mother.

Dear every cretin who took advantage of my mother's generosity: you leeched and you begged for more help than you deserved. You tired her out and she knew she didn't have much time to spend and yet she spent it helping you. You are all cretins and you are shameless.

Dear every lover my mother had: one of your mistresses is gone. You will miss her. If you don't, why was she your lover? If you don't miss her at all my mother was not as wise as I thought her to be. Yes, I'm speaking to you Barry, Barry the Australian who spanked me until I cried and then lied about it to my mother. I kicked you hard in the gonads when I was six and that shut you up. And I'm speaking to you Manuel the architect, the architect who was so possessive and jealous that you pinned my mother to the ground and told her not to move as you tried to make love to her. That was after a party, she told me that, she told me that you were so obsessed and so excessively drunk that you thought she had been unfaithful. You even locked her in the room you were staying in at a certain hotel and she had to wait until you were asleep to grab the keys from your hands and unlock the door and lock it from the outside so that you could not follow her. I'm also talking to you, various slimeballs who took her for granted, condescending pricks who wanted her for her body. It didn't last very long between you because my mother was clever. Did you know she studied at Imperial College in London? Did you know that she taught math at University for years? Do you know she was wiser than you gave her credit for? And did you know she quit working at the University so she could take care of me when I got sick, depressed and paranoid and psychotic? Would you have helped her? Would you have helped her to take care of me? Would you have put her first the way that Vlad did? Is there a better man than Vlad?

Dear every student my mother ever had: my mother told me that she forgot you as soon as she left the classroom. Don't take offense at this. She only remembered one student in particular, a brilliant student apparently, a young man whose name I forget but who would turn up late for class dressed in a leather jacket, too clever to be in class, too sensitive to be told off... you, mysterious student, what was your name and why did you write poetry in class while my mother was talking instead of taking notes like every other good citizen? Was there tension between you, between you and my mother? Where are you now? Where is she now?

Dear very fat man we met on a plane when I was seven: your name was Buddy. You were very friendly to us, to me and my mother and my sister, but you freaked us all out when we later met at a Pizza Hut and I had an ear infection and you helped my mother take me home and then decided that I was possessed. There was no need to shoo my mother out of my room and to begin your stupid incantations, your pleas for mercy from God, our Lord, God Almighty, let this child be, leave this child's body oh Satan, he is young and innocent and sweet. Lord have mercy on him. You are raising your voice now and you are screaming now, Lord leave the boy healthy again and expel the demons from his soul. I am not surprised when my mother kicks you out of the house.

Dear every one of my mother's business associates: as long as you are aware that she went into the business world because of me, because I had been so sick for so long that she couldn't keep up her job at the University, because I was such a burden on her, because she wanted to take care of me while she could and while it was crucial to do so, as long as you are aware that you were not her first choice for company, I forgive you for making her life difficult. I forgive you because I know that the world is run by money and that money is what business is all about and my mother needed money. I know that just because someone is kind and good-natured doesn't mean you can't make their life hell in our capitalist society. And I know that we are all trying to rise to the top. But there was no need to be so forceful about it: there was no need to bully her, to manipulate her, especially when she couldn't come to work because of me. If you want to blame someone then blame me. Also blame me for your failures and for your poverty of spirit, for the rush that you get from failing to accomplish anything, you incompetent and heartless bastards. When my mother discovered that one of you had bugged her office so that you could keep an eye on her, she quit. That is why she quit. Not because the work was too stressful for her, as she told other people. You know very well what I'm talking about, you know that you and your mother were a strange team, and especially you, the creepy middle-aged man who never stopped living with his mother, the man I might have become had my mother not died, you were the only thing she could talk about when she came home from work. But hey, we all have our quirks and yours are just more memorable to me than other people's... the only time that I ever met you, when my mother took me to her office to pick up some papers, I found you very friendly but very strange and I told her so, and that is when she told me all the things that you were up to. Now I know, I know that my mother might simply have been paranoid, but she was not the paranoid type. I also think she was honest. There is no doubt that she was a hard worker and good spirited. In other words, she was not made for your business world. So again, I forgive you, all of you.

Dear old homeless woman my mother used to give my old clothes to: you were very annoying and very talkative and very

very very friendly. You stank of the streets and you talked to the streets when no one else was able to speak to you. You talk so much even now when we bump into each other, whenever I'm back in Portugal. You are such a kind and ugly old woman, and yet there's something beautiful about you, something innocent in your eyes, something fresh about your skin caked with dirt. The rags you always wear used to belong to me, when they weren't rags but rather old sweaters and pajama pants and slippers. My mother must have given you over twenty sweaters over the years. Every Christmas she sought you out and when she found you she asked you to follow her into our house and then she would give you boxes of things that you might need. This made you so happy that you cried. My mother didn't cry, in fact my mother was just irritated by your presence because you spoke so damn much. But she liked you and she never stopped giving you things. And then one day, one Christmas Eve we found you covered in your own piss in the street, and we brought you something to eat, and you cried again. How old are you now? Ninety? Why do you survive, why do you bother to live when life is such shit for you, and people spit at you (and I've seen them do it), and you starve sometimes, almost to death, and you wallow in the dirt and you beg for food and for money and for company? What would my mother have done in your position? My mother often told me when we discussed politics that the only morally right thing to do when your children are starving is to break into a store owned by more than one person and to take enough food for the family. She said the only thing you can do that is worse than killing someone is letting someone die because you are afraid of the law. So dear old homeless lady, you will not die while I am around, not because I care about you, but because it's what my mother would have wanted.

Mother: The flowery dresses that you always wore and the faint smell of lavender emanating from the bathroom whenever you bathed, the joy with which you watched documentaries on animals and the patience with which you walked the dogs while I tried to sleep in, the same silly stories that you told me throughout the years, the stories about your first boyfriend who later became a Marine and the stories that you told other people after you told them to me and I had to listen to them all over again and it bored me, the way you used to say kids kids kids, why do people have children, and I would say you love us really and you would say yes, strangely I do... the patterns in the curtains that you so cherished, the way you insisted that we had to have our meals together and that I had to eat soup before I could chow on my spaghetti, and how you used to name our favorite recipes after us and our pets, the bliss in your eyes the day that you saw me graduate from high school, when I told you I was in love with a girl I had just met, the awkwardness between you and my father at that very graduation ceremony, the pride you claimed to have felt when I gave the graduation speech, the sunlight giving you an even darker complexion than usual, while everybody else seemed paler...

And many things beside. I can remember so much that I had forgotten until your death. Dear mother, this is an experience that everyone must go through and yet it feels unique to me, as though I am the first to have lost a mother. As though your death had forced me to jump into the void, the audient void, and to scream there, to scream to the others and tell them it is okay, it's all okay, we can survive, I am the first and I will be the last to have done this, I am the first to have lost a mother and I'm the last to have known my mother, so you must all take my word for it, you must all believe what I say about my mother because you don't know, you can't know, for she is in the void with us but she is not of the void, she is the void itself. I have fallen into my mother. Into you, your bosom and your hands, your breath and your curly dark hair which, having been a man for some years now, I can tell you was beautiful. You had beautiful thick dark hair, and you were afraid of losing it, with the anemia, the disease and illness and the weakness, the weakness rotting your hair and making it fall. You could have been bald and you still would have been beautiful, and I'm sure that you looked as gorgeous as ever as a corpse, but I can't think of a single reason to think about that. You'll never be a corpse because you are only brain-dead and maybe you can still hear me even if you don't understand, you can hear me and somewhere in that void of a head of yours, you know your son thought you were precious and beautiful and perfect despite every flaw other people saw in you.

Dear everybody who went to my mother's funeral: it was kind of you to come, but you shouldn't have. We wanted a small funeral and instead we had to deal with unwelcome visitors. Thank you for telling us how sorry you were and how you wished you could make things better for us, but we didn't need to hear that. Stop with the pity. Let me and my sister my grandfather and my grandmother and my father deal with our loss. There is no need for you to be here. Go away. Do not look at me to see if I'm crying at my mother's funeral. I am like a character from a novel by Camus: I don't cry at my mother's funeral because I don't feel anything and it is too soon for you to be judging me. Go away. Don't put your hand, your sticky sweaty hand, on my shoulder to reassure me. Don't look at me with those wet eyes, don't tell me how lucky I am to have known her at all, never tell me that she is proud of me even if she isn't here. Just go away. Go back to your stupid house with your stupid family and leave me the hell alone, leave my sister alone, and stop attending funerals to which you weren't invited. Just go away.

Dear woman whose lit cigarette burned a hole through my nylon jacket when I was twelve: my mother got angry at you but it was my fault and your fault, probably mostly your fault, since you were walking without looking where you were going, holding your cigarette out nonchalantly and talking on your cell phone. You seemed like a perfectly stupid woman and that is exactly what my mother said to me after you claimed that I had bumped into you and I claimed that you bumped into me and you threatened to do something that I didn't understand. I remember your face was very skinny, very wrinkled, like a chocolate wrapper. You had dark hair and pale skin, and your eyes scared me. And this was all back when it was okay to smoke inside commercial zones in Portugal. Now we would have been in the right regardless, because you wouldn't have been allowed to smoke in the first place.

Dear fat woman in the park walking her two dogs at night: I called you a cunt and that is what you were. I must've been fourteen then, in love with Rima and angry and silly and on vacation; you were the biggest cunt in the world and your dogs should have been put to sleep after they attacked my Labrador, as though they had never been fed, or petted, or loved. They saw my dog and darted towards us, growling and panting as they neared my dog. I saw the white of their teeth. I am not sorry for kicking them away. They would have killed my dog, lying there on the ground whimpering and yelping. Why would this silly woman not have her dogs on leash, those killer dogs, boxers or something, huge and brown, unless she was mentally retarded? The answer, as you know, is that you are a cunt. And I told you so, once you blamed me for your dogs attacking mine. You said these things happen and I shouldn't have let my dog become such a pushover. You said that I was overreacting and I said you were insane and you said that I should go fuck myself and I told you that you were a cunt. Then I picked my dog up and I took him home and you remained a cunt.

THIRTEEN

Let this all have been a lie. Let my mother be sitting here next to me; let her have been here the whole time.

She is reading the newspaper and stroking the cat, whose fat belly trembles with the purring. My mother's eyes scan the headlines and her fingers turn the pages. The house is very quiet. For lunch we had rice with duck, apple juice and papaya. I told her for the fiftieth time maybe that I don't like papaya but she always forgets. She always forgets that I hate tomato and mango as well, and I pretend to get angry when she serves these things, yet we both know she is a forgetful person. There is no real anger. There is no sadness either. We are happy in the sunlight, out here in the garden, each of us sitting on a deck chair, she's reading, I'm looking at her and thinking: good, good, this is all good.

She survived the operation. A brain hemorrhage kills about 40% of its victims, but my mother wasn't part of that group of unfortunates. My grandfather flew in the best doctor from New York and had him perform the operation. When I arrived from England, weary and panicky, holding my sister's hand, someone said:

"your mother is fine, she is resting, you can see her when she wakes up"

and my father hugged me, and then my grandmother hugged me, and my grandfather and my aunts, and then I hugged my sister. Hugging all around. That's what we needed and I'm glad we got it. My father certainly didn't tell me that she had been declared brain-dead while I was on the plane. We did not walk in silence as we left the airport. There were no tears, because she was alive. We didn't walk towards the car with a sinking in our hearts and he didn't say, in a low, serious voice, that she was brain-dead, and he didn't say that we could only wait and see;

because she was still there.

When she woke, three days later, we were all standing at her side. My sister was the one who noticed that my mother's eyes were open. The nurses were called and I stood back and watched as they adjusted the dials on the machines. She was alive, everything was well, but the moment felt unreal. While everybody else rushed to my mother's line of vision, I stayed where I was and stared. All this panicking, all this waiting and chewing my nails, over at last. Could it be? Was I not going to be motherless after all? I looked at my fingers, my half eaten nails bloody and raw, the scabs and premature wrinkles, and suddenly I could not bear to look back up at my mother, whose eyes were wide open now and looking around. My sister began to cry. My grandmother walked over to me and asked me what was wrong. I said nothing and she said are you sure and I said yes, yes I'm fine.

"just give me a bit of time"

Then my mother spoke. Nobody understood what she said, it was a guttural noise that sounded Russian.

"Sophia, my grandmother said, are you all right, can you hear me, it's me, can you hear me"

and my mother began to nod, and my sister cried some more but I stared on in disbelief.

We took her home a week later. At first my mother remained quiet, but little by little she began to speak more frequently, and by the end of the week she couldn't stop talking. She asked how the cats were, how the dogs were, how her boyfriend Vlad was. We told her everyone was fine and she smiled. When the time came for us to take her home, she had made friends with the nurses and the doctors and other patients. We sat her on a wheelchair and rolled her into the elevator and she meekly waved goodbye to the hospital staff. All she seemed to do was smile. She was frail, yes, but she was well. I had begun to accept my luck, and to love my life again. In the car, driven by Vlad, she spoke of the strange dreams she'd had the night before, dreams of colors and shapes. She had dreamt that she was alone in a world there were no angles. A world without shapes, not shapes the way we are used to thinking of shapes. Everything had form in implication. It was a beautiful dream, she said. We listened and we said nothing. My sister looked at me and smiled, and though I smiled back I knew we were suffering inside, imagining the lonesome days our mother had spent in a sleepless sleep.

When we got home, the dogs squealed and jumped. They smelled her, detecting the scent of the hospital, wagging their tails frenetically and ignoring my orders. I said sit, sit, away, Mathilde, could you get rid of them please? And my sister nodded and took the dogs to the kitchen, locked the door, and returned to us. As the dogs barked and howled my mother said you kept the house very tidy, congratulations, clearly you don't need me around after all, and I said please don't say that, and she said I was only joking. We made her some tea and she drank it slowly, relishing it.

The brain hemorrhage had come unexpectedly and suddenly, but the fact that she had survived it seemed to make my mother more careless than usual. She stopped being a perfectionist and stopped washing dishes immediately after using them, or recycling everything, sending replies to e-mails as soon as she got them... It was good this way. After two weeks at home, I had to return to England, because to miss any more classes would cause problems in the department. I made Vlad promise to take care of her. I made her promise to take care of herself, to avoid stress and to do exactly what she wanted, not to allow herself to be bullied into doing other people's bidding for once. She agreed. She said I love you and I said I love you too, and then Vlad drove me to the airport.

Although my mother is well, I am forever worried that something will happen to her again. What if she falls? What if she cuts her fingers with a knife, and begins to panic? What if the dogs knock her over in their overzealous way? What if she gets mugged? There is no peace anymore, everything's a risk. But she is alive. She reads the newspaper, goes online, watches movies in Russian, feeds the birds, calls my grandmother every day, and has taken up doing crossword puzzles. She's good at them, and she never asks for help. She loves the sunlight and she loves me and everyone else. Somehow she's childish now, innocent, even more naïve than before, and we love her all the more.

One day my father comes to visit. He and my mother have not had a long conversation in years, but his presence during the days when she was asleep has proven his good nature. When he arrives, she greets him warmly and they sit on the couch and talk. They discuss the past, the present, their relationships. My father admits to having been very very concerned, and to have come straight away to see her at the hospital. My mother says she's grateful that he took care of us. They begin to reminisce. They call me and my sister and they start to tell us anecdotes, stories from the past: the time that my sister kicked me during her sleep and I complained and they didn't believe me and then my sister did it again and I woke up again and I complained again and they still didn't believe me, but the third time they saw it happen and they moved me to another bed. The time that I began to cry for no reason and my mother wanted to give me a dummy and my father said he's too old for a dummy, and my mother said give him a dummy. So my father gave me a dummy and I shut up. The time I had a little accident in the bath, or maybe it was my sister, they can't really remember. The time they spent at my grand-father's farm shortly after their marriage, living free. The time that they spent in France, living freer. The time my grandmother accidentally used sand instead of breadcrumbs to make lunch and my father politely said it was very nice. My sister and I listen, and we smile and we nod. Everything is good.

And the night of January 3rd, 2010, I hear my mother whisper to my sister that the time has nearly come. Because I don't want them to think I was eavesdropping, I don't ask what the time has come for. I remain seated on the couch in the living room, and I listen. My sister says:

"are you sure"

and my mother says "yes"

"but how will we tell him"

and my mother says "we won't tell him, we will just have to show him"

and my sister begins to cry. No tears have been shed in this house since my mother came back from the hospital, and the sound is strange. It is as though my sister were choking on something. I get up and I walk to the kitchen, where my mother's hands are tightly wrapped around my sister's neck and her thumbs press deep into her veins.

"what are you doing" I say

and my mother looks at me and says:

"you have to know, you have to see"

"what do I have to see"

"you have to see me for the demon that I am"

"what are you talking about"

She says "look at me, look carefully, look at my eyes and my skin, am I really your mother"

"yes"

"are you sure" she says

"yes of course I'm sure, you're my mother, stop strangling her, stop, it mom, what are you doing, stop it"

But my mother doesn't let go, so I take my mother's arms and bend them around, and my mother screams and lets go of my sister, who gasps for air and crouches on the floor.

"what's wrong with you" I say.

But my mother doesn't answer. Instead she begins to scream and the scream is endless, a high-pitched thing ripping out of her throat so loudly that I go deaf for a moment. Then, still screaming, she looks at me with eyes a little too big, a little too deep, the quietest eyes I have ever seen and a shocking contrast to her open mouth. It is as though the top half of her face is immobile, a painting almost — the lower half is animated by some demonic force entirely beyond her control. My mother's arms are raised by this demon, and with a plop they fall onto the floor. The same happens with her legs: they simply give way and collapse. Yet her torso and her head remain hovering in the air, her eyes are transfixed on me, and I grab my sister's hand and we run together out of the house and into the night. We make our way past our neighbors' houses, past the gates and the doors and the swimming pool, until we are by the road that leads to Lisbon. Here we pause for breath and my sister says:

"what's happening to mommy"

and I say "why did she say that the time has come, what did she mean by that"

and my sister says "I don't know you're talking about"

"come on, tell me"

and she says "no, I really don't know what you're talking about"

and I say "Jesus Christ"

"what"

and I say "I heard you and mom speaking, and she said something about the time having come"

and my sister says "I have no idea, I have no idea, what's happening to mommy"

"I don't know, I just don't know"

Was it a dream? Am I dreaming, and if so: when will I wake up? And at once I grow convinced that it has been a dream, that everything is okay, and that I should take my sister back home. She says:

"no please no please"

and I say "we have to, her arms have fallen off, and her legs, we must take care of our mother"

So we walk back towards the house, holding hands, in total silence. We find our mother's pieces on the kitchen floor. Her head has separated from her body and lies in a corner. Her hands hold each other. Her legs, one next to the head and one on the table, quiver slightly. The torso is missing, and we look for it for a few minutes before realizing that the dogs are playing with it upstairs. We attempt to reassemble our mother, silently and diligently, but this proves difficult. For starters, because there is no blood at all in her body, we are thoroughly terrified, and so our hands tremble. There is also the fact that we are almost out of tape, we have no staples, and neither of us knows how to knit or sew. To assemble the pieces, therefore, we have to be particularly careful not to waste our duct tape. We place our mother's pieces on the table in the living room, and begin with the head, which we attach to the neck carefully, holding back tears, and using only a little duct tape, as little as we can. Then we attach the arms, surprisingly heavy arms for such a small woman, and then the legs. Now we see we have more duct tape than we thought, we reinforce the area connecting the head to the torso, it seems to be the most fragile area. And our mother is reassembled, we dress her up again and sit her on the couch, and we wait for something to happen. The dogs are happy to see their mother again, but they are suspicious as well, as if they know that something has changed in her. After a few minutes, my mother's eyes open and she looks at me, her lips begin to move, and I hear the words:

"you killed me"

"I didn't kill you" I say,

and my sister says "who are you talking to"

and I say "didn't you hear her"

"no, hear who"

"mom just spoke, she said that I killed her"

and my sister says "that is just stupid"

But now my mother has come back to life, and her hands begin to move, and she raises one finger and puts it to her mouth and goes *shhhhh*. My sister jumps up and yelps, and I say "what the hell, what the hell is happening to her"

and my sister says "oh mommy mommy"

and I say "Jesus Christ, Jesus Christ, mother, what happened to you"

and here my mother turns her head, slowly but also clumsily, and says: You killed me. You killed me. You killed me.

FOURTEEN

No, I didn't kill you.

If I had killed you, I would have nothing to write about. I'd already have committed every mistake, burned down every bridge, dismissed every memory I have of you as a facsimile.

If I had been born or made so self-destructive that the only thrill left was the murder of my mother — I hope you'd have murdered me first. You could have smothered me at any moment: in my crib, where I slept silently for the few two weeks of my life ("you only started crying at night on Christmas Day"), or in my bed, where I slept angry and confused until I was twelve and you let me go to boarding school. You could have asked Vlad, your lover, to use the sniping techniques he learned in the Ukraine to wipe me out in a second.

You saw the good in me, as I still see the good in you. Now that you're anywhere but here, and life has resumed its precarious infinite flux, I sit around a lot. I sit and sleep. When I'm not sleeping, I'm doing things mostly as I did them when you were alive; except I no longer feel I need your permission. You were a liberal mother. You protected me too much, then too little when I grew up. Then, when you stopped protecting me at all, when I stood there at your grave with my sister and it was up to me to comfort her, I finally accepted how hopelessly vanished you were. That was your adjective, and still is, and will be for the rest of everyone's life: vanished.

You used to quote a few poems every once in a while. I have them all here. Some, you sent to me while I was still in my little boarding school. Others you just quoted so often that I still remember them. These poems have helped me define you in my mind. You went for simplicity, for a mix of levity and subtle darkness, for little aphorisms. That was you as a human being, as a woman and as a mother: simple, light in every way, wise. You cared nothing for Yeats's widening gyres, because you had found your Yeats:

I'm looking for the face I had
Before the world was made.

You were obsessively feminine, but never girly. With the money you might have inherited someday, you hoped to found a center for helping immigrants in Portugal. That was your face before the world was made, the world of facades and pretensions and hand-shaking and correctness: you had the face of unintimidating kindness. You smiled when something was funny to you, and sometimes you laughed alone. You liked to laugh. You never laughed very much.

You said the only poem that would remain forever relevant to you was one by Victor Hugo: a poem he'd written for his dead daughter. And when Hugo describes walking alone, unknown, his back curved, his hands crossed, to his daughter's grave, I see myself in his shoes, and you in Leopoldine's eternal bed.

When I wanted to go to India to help the poor, you reminded me to clean my room as well, because charity starts at home.

You told me the story of the Portuguese noblewoman murdered in front of her child by three men. And, perhaps to instill some humility in me from the start, you didn't say she was the lover, illegitimate and ill fated, of a prince. You didn't tell me, the first time you told this story, a true story for the most part, a part of our tiny Portuguese culture, that the prince, when he heard of the murder, vowed to find the men, to slaughter them, to rip their hearts out because they didn't need hearts, to exhume the body of his lover when she had at last been avenged and have her seated on the throne that ought to have been hers and made all of us, the outside world, the lesser people kiss her skeletal hand. And he succeeded. You had no reason to give me these details when what bothered you the most, what shocked and roused you from the sleep of life without stories was the murder of a woman in front of her child. That was unforgivable. That gruesome and forever unacknowledged, never emphasized point — that men could drag a child into the carnage — trumped all other aspects of the tragedy. And it was a tragedy, the kind of sordid tale that delights the operagoers, and so many operas have come out of that affair; but how many people have thought through the child's head? That was why you didn't care to mention that this business of love and revenge was the crucial part in the minds of men and later of men and women, who had begun to exist when you were a child and of whom you formed the vanguard with your refusal to compromise what you thought were your duties as a mother and friend to your own children. You who didn't care about the star-crossed lovers or the plucked-out hearts of the men who'd forced them from each other, whose passion lay in the neglected detail of the little one staring as the decapitation of its mother passed it by like so many other terrible things except that this one was forever to mark it and haunt and consume it. The decapitation of the mother.

You forgave me all my failings. I never had to forgive you for anything, except the time you grabbed my wrist too violently to calm me down and one of your nails dug into my flesh and drew blood.

You owe me one drop of blood.

Let this be the final fistful of earth I loose upon your coffin. I know where your tomb lies. I'll visit you soon.

zero
books

Contemporary culture has eliminated both the concept of the public and the figure of the intellectual. Former public spaces – both physical and cultural – are now either derelict or colonized by advertising. A cretinous anti-intellectualism presides, cheerled by expensively educated hacks in the pay of multinational corporations who reassure their bored readers that there is no need to rouse themselves from their interpassive stupor. The informal censorship internalized and propagated by the cultural workers of late capitalism generates a banal conformity that the propaganda chiefs of Stalinism could only ever have dreamt of imposing. Zer0 Books knows that another kind of discourse – intellectual without being academic, popular without being populist – is not only possible: it is already flourishing, in the regions beyond the striplit malls of so-called mass media and the neurotically bureaucratic halls of the academy. Zer0 is committed to the idea of publishing as a making public of the intellectual. It is convinced that in the unthinking, blandly consensual culture in which we live, critical and engaged theoretical reflection is more important than ever before.